A View of Croydon

Postcards from the Past

Inside Front Cover (Left)
These four postcards show churches which have been demolished in the latter 20th century, mostly because they need expensive repairs and congregations have fallen.

New Wesleyan Church, West Croydon about 1904 (Top left)
This was in London Road, almost opposite Croydon General Hospital.

Baptist Church, South Norwood about 1905 (Top right)
This was in Oliver Grove and has been replaced by a modern structure.

Addiscombe Wesleyan Church about 1904 (Bottom left)
This stood in Lower Addiscombe Road until destroyed by fire soon after the Second World War. Published by Stengel.

Wesleyan Church, South Norwood about 1903 (Bottom right)
This stood on South Norwood Hill opposite The Stanley Halls. Opened in 1875 it closed and was demolished for structural reasons in the late 1970s. Published in Field's Art series.

Contents

Page

Editor - **John Gent**

Assistant Editors - **Ken Harman**
Roger Packham

Published by CNHSS - Croydon Natural History and Scientific Society
96a Brighton Road, South Croydon, Surrey CR2 6AD

ISBN: 978-0-906047-25-5
Printed by Gemini Press, Shoreham-by-Sea (01273) 464884
96 pages 378 illustrations

April 2011

Front Cover

Top centre
This is a 'FAB' card with a silk centrepiece (in this example the Croydon Coat of Arms). It was intended that the recipient could remove the side pieces and use the silk centrepiece as a patchwork piece.

Lower left
Card sold to raise funds for Croydon General Hospital.

Lower right
St. Michael's Church, Croydon about 1905
This fine church was designed by the famous architect, John Loughborough Pearson and was intended to have a tall spire but funds were insufficient. It is still a well-known landmark in the town. Published by Pritchards, North End, Croydon.

Back Cover

Picturesque Surrey - Croydon from Mitcham Common (Top left)
About 1903. A Tuck's Oilette series card.

East Croydon Station - 2008 (Centre)
Croydon Tramlink's new livery is seen outside the 1980s station. Modern card published by John Bradshaw (Transport of Delight).

The Pond, Bradmore Green Coulsdon about 1907 (Lower left)
Over a hundred years later, this view is virtually unchanged in 2010. It is now a Conservation Area. Published in Field's Surrey Series.

£10.95

NEW THORNTON HEATH
Thornton Heath
SELHURST PARK
NORWOOD
Norwood Junct.
The Grove
Thornton Ho.
Cricket Ground
Lon. Parcels Delv. Comp.
WEST
SOUTH
Selhurst
Selhurst Wood
ENMORE PARK
Union Workhouse
Croydon Infirmary
Croydon Cemetery
Cricket Ground
WARD
NORTH PARK
WOODSIDE
Windmill Road
Waddonmarsh
St James's Road
West Croydon
Addiscombe Road
Factory Lane
Gasometer
Filter Works
CROYDON
CENTRAL
British Sch.
Slaughter House
East Croydon
New Croydon
Upper Addiscombe Road
WADDON
Hare & Hounds
Vicarage Road
Waddon Lo.
Waddon House
Church St.
George Street
Fair Field
WARD
Parkhill
Friends Meeting Ho.
Waddon
Duppas Hill Road
Duppas Hill
Cricket Ground
Coombe Lane
Coombe Road
Coldharbour
Warham Rd.
South Croydon
London Brighton & South Coast Railway
Croham Rd.
Croham Lane
Croham Farm
Haling Park
SOUTH
WARD
Selsdon Rd
Violet Lane

INTRODUCTION

This publication is the ninth in the CNHSS series of illustrated local histories. It demonstrates for one town the great variety of picture postcards published since the end of the 19th century. The first postcards were issued in Austria in 1869 and the first British postcard was issued in 1870. Initially these were plain official cards embossed with a ½ d stamp. This was half the letter rate, and as they cost only a ½ d there were complaints from the stationery trade. As a result a charge of 6½ d per dozen was introduced in 1872 and the cards were sold only in this way.

Soon anyone was allowed to produce postcards but they had to look like the official cards, but without the coat of arms, and anything could be written or printed on the back, but nothing apart from the address on the front. After printing the cards had to be sent to the Inland Revenue to have a ½ d stamp printed or embossed on them.

There was a Victorian view that the postcard was vulgar and comments were made about the absurdity of writing private information on an open piece of card which might be read by half a dozen people before it reached its destination. Nevertheless the popularity of postcards increased and from 1894 the production and use of privately printed cards was permitted, with the use of an adhesive stamp. Many included small pictures but the address side had to be clear. From 1902 the Divided Back postcard was introduced allowing the message and address to appear on one side with a full illustration on the other. The great boom in sending and collecting cards was then at its peak. Many were attractively coloured and printed in Germany which already had an expert printing industry. Real photographic cards printed on a Rotary Press had by now arrived and these in particular are eagerly sought by collectors. They form a valuable social and topographical record of a period of great change.

Postcards covered every imaginable subject from aviation to zoos. Competition between publishers, many of them small local firms, saw up to the minute views of local events. For example an early morning train crash at East Croydon Station was photographed and a postcard was on sale and posted the same afternoon.

In effect, between 1900 and 1912 the postcard was the equivalent of the tabloid newspaper and telephone combined. Newspapers had few if any photographs in the Edwardian years. By 1914 800 million cards were sent annually in the UK and there were up to six or seven postal collections and deliveries each day. Messages such as “meet me at the station at 5.00pm today” were common and could almost always be relied upon to be delivered on time.

The First World War stemmed the flow of imported cards and in 1918 the postage rate was increased to 1d. The telephone was becoming more common and the ‘golden age’ of postcards was over. Local view postcards continued in production until the 1980s but the number and variety fell dramatically. Today, apart from in tourist areas, it is often difficult to find local postcard views, although some are produced by local societies and individuals.

The picture postcard is an invaluable record of a time of great change in our villages, towns and cities from the Edwardian period onwards and helps us to piece together their development, often providing the only known record of buildings, streets, people and events as demonstrated in the following pages.

CROYDON

Croydon grew up just to the north of an important gap and series of dry valleys through the North Downs which reach their highest and widest just south of the town. At the beginning of the 19th century Croydon was a small but important market town with a population of about 6,000. Transport improvements, better drainage and a good water supply led to its growing popularity as a commuter town and by the end of the century it was a County Borough with a population of around 130,000. It included the growing districts of Upper and South Norwood, Norbury, Thornton Heath, Selhurst, Addiscombe, Woodside, Shirley, Waddon and part of Purley. There was plenty of local employment in agriculture, breweries, transport, service and small factories. Addington, Coulsdon and Sanderstead with their medieval churches were remote rural communities, the combined population of the three parishes totalling only about 8,000.

Large areas of open countryside remained within the area and rural activities co-existed with the developing suburban life of the new residents. The 20th century brought great changes as the motor vehicle became more reliable. Districts such as Shirley, Sanderstead, Selsdon and Coulsdon which were some distance from railway stations could be reached by the expanding network of motor bus routes. As a result housing development spread to the higher areas, previously difficult to reach. Gradually much of the remaining countryside was covered by new housing and by the 1930s almost unbroken urban development linked Croydon to London.

A new Green Belt policy had placed more control on development but there was some expansion of and within the urban areas after the Second World War. In the 1950s Croydon Council produced a new plan for the town centre and encouraged large-scale office development which transformed the area and brought more local employment. In 1965 The Greater London Council was established and this absorbed the former County Borough and adjacent southern areas including Coulsdon, Sanderstead and Selsdon into the new London Borough of Croydon. Changes since then have seen the loss of local industries and an increasing ethnic diversity in the population. Despite it now being regarded as part of London the town still maintains the air of an independent provincial town with its long history and its own life and activities.

Extract from Bacon’s map of Croydon about 1890 (left)

This map shows the town of Croydon at the end of the 19th century and early in the postcard era still surrounded by fields, farms and woods. Off the map are still rural Norbury, with growing Upper and South Norwood to the north. The Norwood Hills rise to a height of 376ft (115 metres) above sea level. Addiscombe, Woodside and Shirley to the east remained mainly rural. The open downland to the south beyond Purley, Sanderstead, Selsdon, and Coulsdon was just beginning to see new housing development. The land here reaches a height of 570 feet (174 metres) above sea level, the town centre of Croydon being at a height of 170 feet (52 metres) above sea level.

At the time this map was published, the Central Croydon branch railway had just closed. The track is still shown but the new Town Hall would be built in Katharine Street on the site of the station and opened in 1896.

Scale approximately 4 inches (10 cm) to the mile.

Official Postcard - 1870 style

An early official postcard with crest and printed stamp, sent from South Norwood on 4 February 1875.

CROYDON POSTCARDS & THEIR PUBLISHERS

1890s Court card - above

This is the earliest known postcard of Croydon. Presumably it was produced in 1896 or 1897 just after the new Town Hall opened. If it was later it is unlikely the 189 date would have been included. Publisher not known.

1890s postally used Court card - below

This is the earliest known Croydon view card to be posted locally. It was produced by Bender and Lewis. The firm also produced cards of other parts of the country.

The approximate equivalent Pre-Decimal and Decimal currency is as follows:
½d (half penny) = ¼p (value perhaps equivalent to 80p today)
1d (one penny) = ½p
6d (six pence) = 2½p
1 shilling = 5p

Nearly all early coloured cards of the late 19th and early 20th century were produced and printed in Germany even if they were for local publishers. By the early years of the 20th century a large number of local publishers had appeared on the scene virtually everywhere. There is some difficulty in defining 'Publishers' because some large companies produced postcards for local shops including the name of the shop, but omitting their own name. As real photographic cards became more common from the early 1900s many were produced by or for local photographers who worked mainly from their homes, or, if they were professional photographers, from their studios.

The collection of the Editor of this publication now contains around 8,000 cards of the present London Borough of Croydon. These were produced by about 300 publishers as listed on pages 7 and 8. Page 6 includes details of a few of the principal local publishers.

The early 'Court Sized' cards were published mainly between 1895 and 1898. These were 3½ inches by 4½ inches and were superceded between about 1894 and 1900 by the 'Intermediate Sized' cards, measuring about 3 inches by 5 inches. Postal Union sized cards measuring 3½ inches by 5½ inches followed from 1898 for much of the 20th century but larger cards of varying measurements have become more common in recent years (see pages 90 to 96).

The 'Golden Age' of postcards was from 1900 until the First World War. This was a period of great change. In Croydon the electric tramway between the borough boundaries at Norbury and Purley, together with several local branches provided an easy and relatively cheap means of travel. In 1908 the LCC (London County Council) trams reached Norbury and south Londoners could change there and continue out to the foothills of the North Downs at Purley. Places such as Riddlesdown and Farthing Downs (Coulsdon) had very large tearooms which could cater for Sunday School Treats and hordes of day visitors. The nearer recreation grounds and parks nearly all had bandstands and provided brass band concerts until the 1950s. Scenic attractions such as Croham Hurst and Shirley (more correctly called Addington) Hills were also increasingly visited. Postcards of these attractions have survived in large numbers as have those of local chapels and churches. However the great majority of local views remain in much smaller quantities, possibly because they were produced and sold in much smaller numbers. The salvage drives of the Second World War may also partially account for this.

The period after the First World War is much less well-covered but it should be noted that home produced photographs were often printed with a postcard backing which is probably why many postcards do not have proper captions. Messages can be very interesting and often reveal out-dated forms of address and record local events of the time, such as Zeppelin raids, Suffragette meetings and visits to local places of entertainment.

The first day of electric trams in Croydon

This card is notable as being the first known view of a local Croydon event, although it was not in fact used until two years later. It shows the scene at West Croydon on September 26th 1901, and appears to have been photographed from upstairs in The Railway Bell public house on the corner of Tamworth Road. North End is to the right and London Road to the left. At this time the main entrance to West Croydon station was behind the trees to the left, the building being just visible. There were no buildings on the bridge until a rebuilding in the 1930s. The electric trams replaced a smaller horse-tram system and the main route from Norbury to Purley seen here survived until 1951. Publisher not known.

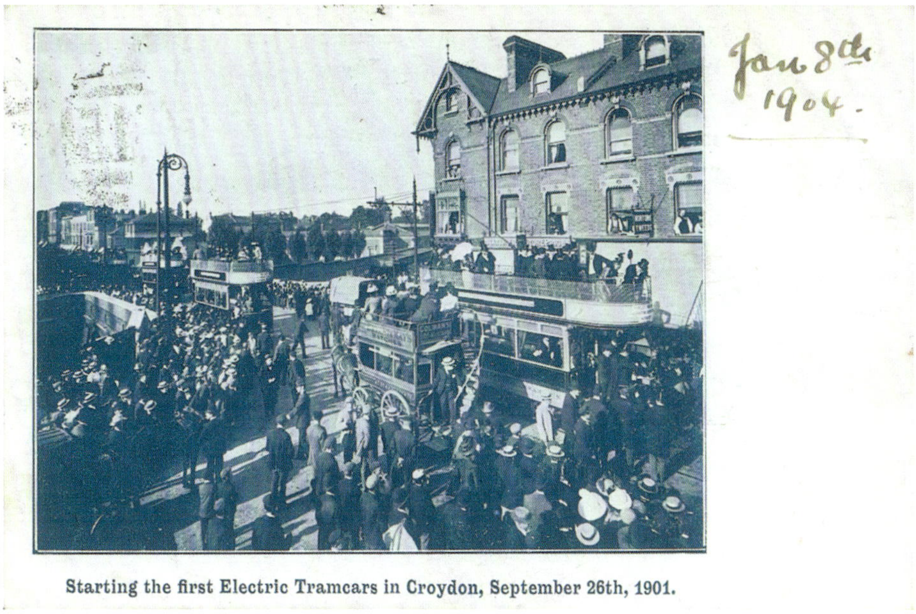

Roffey and Clark's Printing Works and Library/Shop about 1906

The firm had started in 1880 when Harry Clark joined Mr Roffey to take over the existing bookselling and printing business of Francis Warren in the High Street. With the rebuilding of this area, a new shop was opened in 1894 and the firm traded here until 1962 when it was acquired by the adjacent Grant Bros.

The printing works were linked to the main shop in High Street by a bridge across Middle Street. The High Street premises provided a good bookshop as seen in the lower picture.

The door leading to the bridge is in the background. The tables in the foreground have prominent displays of postcard albums and there is a quite extensive library.

W.H.Smith and Boots provided similar libraries until after the Second World War. A small charge was made for the loan of books.

Roffey & Clark produced a number of local view postcards, some as the R&C Series and presumably they were printed in these works. Both cards were produced by the firm.

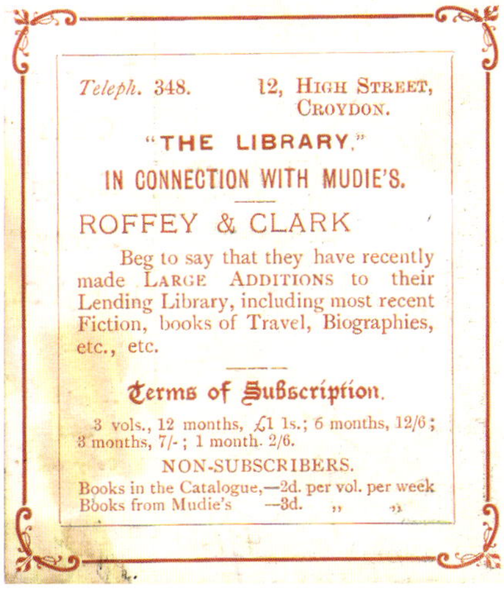

Teleph. 348. 12, HIGH STREET, CROYDON.

"THE LIBRARY."

IN CONNECTION WITH MUDIE'S.

ROFFEY & CLARK

Beg to say that they have recently made LARGE ADDITIONS to their Lending Library, including most recent Fiction, books of Travel, Biographies, etc., etc.

Terms of Subscription.

3 vols., 12 months, £1 1s.; 6 months, 12/6; 3 months, 7/- ; 1 month. 2/6.

NON-SUBSCRIBERS.

Books in the Catalogue,—2d. per vol. per week
Books from Mudie's —3d. „ „

PRINCIPAL CROYDON PUBLISHERS OF LOCAL CARDS

BENDER & LEWIS 1897 to 1914

JOSEPH BENDER was a German local photographer who formed the Velograph Syndicate in 1897. This combined film making and production of a number of early 'Court' sized postcards of various parts of the country. (Croydon example at foot of page 4). The Syndicate failed and by 1899 Bender had joined forces with **THOMAS LEWIS**, another local photographer. Their premises were at 126 George Street but by 1903 they had additional premises at 242 London Road. The adjacent premises at number 244 had by 1908 become home to **THE PHOTO PRINTING & PUBLISHING COMPANY** which seems to have been Bender's firm. Lewis took the photographs and continued to do so into the 1920s after Bender had left, presumably in 1914 because he was a German National.

BATCHELDER BROTHERS

BERTRAM BATCHELDER first produced a few printed postcards around 1907 but by 1908 was established as BATCHELDER BROTHERS at 106 George Street. The firm was described as a Wholesale Stationers and was publishing some fine sepia photographic cards. It is likely that Batchelders worked with Benders as a large number of real photographic cards bearing the name or logo of Batchelder as publisher were published until around 1916. These covered many parts of the country and were probably produced by The Photo Printing & Publishing Company. That company went into receivership in 1922 and by then Batchelder Brothers had moved to London Road but appear to have been trading as a wholesale stationers and no more postcards appeared.

P & A BUCHANAN

12 Queenswood Avenue, Thornton Heath. This firm produced good quality photographic cards mostly without captions. They specialised in school and other buildings countrywide.

WILLIAM T. COOK

21 Alexandra Road, Croydon - approx 1908 to 1913 then Westway, Caterham-on-the-Hill and finally Acme Works, Chaldon Road, Caterham-on-the-Hill

WILLIAM T. COOK was a photographer who at least initially worked from home. He photographed and published a large number of real photographic postcards, many recording local side-streets and a few events. Unfortunately most have faded, presumably due to poor fixing. In latter days he sold his Rotary Printing Press to Ken Carr of Pamlin Prints. This was set up at the Photomatic works in Potters Bar and is thought to have gone to the Museum in Bradford.

WILLIAM H. DRAKE

2 Ecclesbourne Road, Thornton Heath (previously at Earlsfield)

Between about 1920 and 1930 he produced high quality real photographic cards of the area from Croydon 15 miles south along the Kent and Surrey borders. These provide a particularly useful record of areas that underwent development in that period when fewer postcards were being published. For examples see pages 68 and 69.

WILLIAM A. FIELD

33 Selhurst Road, South Norwood (later 35 as well)

WILLIAM A. FIELD was a wholesale stationers and traded from around 1899 to 1919. The firm produced an excellent series of coloured cards of Croydon and the areas to the south. A number of these are reproduced on pages 19 to 30.

O. J. MORRIS

168 (later renumbered to 304) Beulah Hill, Upper Norwood, SE19. He was a transport enthusiast and photographer who produced very high quality sepia postcards between 1919 and 1959. They included handwritten notes on the back and he published lists. He was a very private man and was known as 'the man in black'. He died in 1961.

CHARLES HARRISON PRICE

66A North End, Croydon (c1906 -1946)
36 George Street, Croydon (c1913 -1927) 62 High Street, Croydon (c1926-1946)

C.H. PRICE was a photographer who published a large quantity of high quality real photographic postcards. The Editor of this publication has over 1,500 different views in his collection. Many are in numbered series and the gaps in the collection indicate that he probably produced about 3,000 different views in total. He used a large format glass-plate camera. For many years he lived with his sister in Hathaway Road but latterly often stayed overnight working at his High Street studio. He was found dead there in 1946 due to a gas leak. His sister was not concerned that he had not been home for several days as this was quite common.

SURREY FLYING SERVICES

Croydon Airport from about 1920 until 1939

CAPTAIN MUIR and C. GRANT based at Croydon Airport where they owned and based several aircraft. They organised pleasure flights over London and produced an excellent series of aerial view postcards in the 1920s covering much of southern England in the SFS SERIES. They also produced a few topographical postcards.

PAMLIN PRINTS 73 Temple Road, Croydon and later 55A Coombe Road, Croydon.

KENNETH CARR founded Pamlin Prints, deriving the name from his wife, PAM and son, COLIN. He was a transport enthusiast and good photographer who had a great interest in old photographs. Initially he issued monthly lists and sold hand-printed copies to order. In the 1960s a discussion with the Editor of this publication encouraged him to start producing postcards and in the following years he produced a vast quantity of real photographic postcards. Many of these were for libraries and museums. Rising costs led him to change to lithographic reproduction which was not then as good as now. He was not satisfied with the results so reverted to hand-printing photographs to order.
A visit to his premises in Coombe Road showed what it must have been like in many of the early postcard publishers homes. Piles of photographs lay around, there were boxes and packages of cards awaiting distribution. and a general air of chaos. Ken's welcoming cup of tea was invariably generously laced with whisky! For examples of his postcards see page 88. He died in 1996.

List of Publishers known to have published Croydon views

This may not be a complete list but has been put together by examining all the cards in the collection of the Editor of this publication. Some of those listed published quite a lot of local cards and some very few. Of particular note for the quality of their postcards from those not listed above are Blanche, Croydon Times, Reval, Symes and Talba. Many of the names listed are of retail establishments.

A.C. Series, TH
A.E.S. & Co, London
AH.S. Series
A.S.
A.S. Series
AC Series, Purley
Ace series, The
ACLA Series
ACR Series
Adamstone Series
Addington Co-operative Society
Aerial Photographic Co., London
Aero Films & Aero Pictorial
Aero Series, Hendon
Agutter Series
Air Views Ltd.
AJB Series
AJS Series
Aldridge, Station Road, SN
Alexandra Series - Talbot, UN
All Nations Bible College, UN
Allders Series
Allison Series
Allworth Photos
Alumino Registered
Arcade Series, The
Arno's Series
Artistic Publishing Co., London
Atkins, T., UN

B.S.S., TH
B.S.W. & Co. "Ancto" Series
Bakers Series
Barber, C. & G., Kenley
Bartlett, John
Batchelder Bros.
Baxter, Florence
Beach Series
Beagles, J.
Bedford Lemére, London
Bell Series, Leigh on Sea
Bender & Lewis
Bennett, A.J.
Berch Series
Beresford, TH
Black, H, TH
Black's
Blake Series
Blanche, Brighton Road
Bonds Series
Bookery Series
Boots
Bourne Society, The
Bradshaw, John
Bridge House, Real Photo Series
Bronshaw's
Buchanan, P. & A.
Bunce Bros., Caterham
Burdekin, W.H.
Burgess, F.H.
Butcher, Co, Anerley Road

C. E. C.
C4
Cabman Bros.
Cameron, D. & A.
Canon Series
Card House
Cardcraft Publishing Service, London
Carey, J.T.
Caterham Printing Works
Chick, Croydon
Clark & Mann, Duke Street, Strand
Clark & Norman Ltd., London
Clayton & Sons, Woodside Green
Clayton's Series
Close & Cole, Beckenham
CNHSS (Croydon Natural History & Scientific Society)
Cole's Series, J., Kenley
Collins, E. Norton, SN
Commercial & General Photographic Co., London
Compton Stationer, UN
Cook, J.H.
Cook, W.T. (W.T.C Series)
Coombe Wood Restaurant
Cox, Waiter, WaBington
Croft's Series
Croll, J.A.
Croydon Airport Society
Croydon Museum and Arts
Croydon Press Office
Croydon Public Libraries
Croydon Series
Croydon Times, (The C.T. Series)
Custom Cards & Gifts

Daniell
Davies Series
Davis Photo Series
Deacock's Emporium, SN
Dean, J.J. & Sons
Dennis, E.T.W. & Sons, Scarborough
Deverell, Sharpe & Gibson Ltd.
Diplock Series
Drake, W.H.
Dunn, A.S., UN

Eade
Elliott and Fry
Enfield, B.S.
English & Buckingham
Everitt, T.H., UN
Evezard, E.G.
EWH
Excel Series
Exchange Series, The, London Road

Farmery, A.M.
Farrier, A.K, TH
Fenell, G.
Fenske, E.
Field, W.A.
Flint, Albert, Camberwell
Ford, Norman
Frampton's, Warlingham Green
French & Co., Wallington
Fricker J.H. UN
Friend Smith
Frith, Francis & Co. Ltd.
Fry, B.H., Brighton
FWH

G.C.L.A. Series
Gale, W.
Gardener, W.
Garnham, E.
George & Kennie
GHS
Gilley, Stationer, South End
Godfrey, R. H., Kenley
Goodwin Series
Gosden's
Gourd Series
Grinstead, H.F., Caterharn and South Croydon
Grocock, A.
Grubb, H.R.
Gundry, A, SN
Guy's Series

Hadaways, Addiscombe

Halsted, C.E., UN
Handford, Archie
Hardy, A.E., TH
Hartmann, Frederick, London
Harvey, L.R.
Haynes of Dulwich
Hedger, Fred. A, West Norwood
Hill, Mrs. T.H., Kenley
Hill's Photo Series
Hinton, Leslie
Hodgson, H., Whyteleafe
Holloway, Addiscombe
Homeland
Hossack, A., Croydon
Howes Series
Hurst Series, TH

Imperial Series

J. Bros., Croydon
Jakson, Woodcote
John's
Jones, P.R., SN
Judges Ltd., Hastings

K. & S. Series, TH
K.B. Sunbeam Regd.
Kerr, M.W., NOR
Keystone Art Co. Ltd., SN
King, E.
King, Howard M.
Knight Collection, The
Knight, A.S.
Knight, 1., Old Lodge Lane
Knowles "Addiscombe" Series

Landerer & Brown, (L & B Surrey View Series)
Lansdowne Studio, The, Kenley
Laver, G.R.
Lee, Streatham
Leisten, G. & C., Coulsdon
Levy, Louis, (LL)
Lilywhite
Locomotive Publishing Co.
London View Co. Ltd., The
Lufkins, Post Office, Brighton Road

Mackworth, Wickham Avenue
Maclean, H.
Marks Series
Marriott's Photo Stores, Hastings
Marris & Revene
Marsh's Series
Martin, Charles
Mason's "Alpha" Series
Maximum Original
Middleton, H.
Milton "Gazette" Series, London
Misch & Stock
Moore's, F. Railway Photographs
Morgan & Co., Selhurst
Morgan, H., Purley
Morris, O.J.
Mossack, A.

Newton & Gutteridge, TH
Nicholls, Anerley
Nicholls, UN
Norbury Series
Norbury Studio
Norfolk Printing Plant, London
Norfolk Printing, London
Norman's
North Cheam Bookshop
Novelty Post Card Co., Liverpool

Oliver, M.G.

Pamlin Prints
Pan Aero Pictures, Kingston on Thames
Parsons, Will
Pathé Frères
Peckham, H.
Photo Printing & Publishing Co.
Photochrom Company Ltd., The
Pledger, C., TH
Pollard Series
Poole, W.A., NOR
Popular Series, The
Post Office, Godstone Road
Pouteau, E.
Powell Series
Premier Photo Co., Croydon
Price, C.H. (CHP)
Priestley & Co.
Pritchard XL Series
Proctor's Series
Promise
Purley Bazaar & Library
Pyne, Croydon

Q & C Series
Qualis Photo Co.
Quarton & Chivers, The Exchange, Purley

R. A. (Postcards). Ltd, London
R.A.P. Co., London
Ragged School Union & Shaftesbury Society, London
Rapid Photo Printing Co., London
Real Photo Postcards K.B. Ltd. (Sunbeam)
Real Photo Series - (R.A. Sellwood)
Redmond, C.J.
Redmond's Library
Reval Series
Rextone
Riches Series
Ridout Publisher, Anerley
Ringer & Sons, Warlingham
Rival Photographic Series, The
Robertson
Robertson Series
Robertson, J.R.
Robinson, P.W., London
Roffey & Clark, Croydon
Rogers, W.H. Croydon and SN
Rohan et Cie
Rolls, A.E. Series
Rotary Photographic Co. Ltd., The
Routter Series
RTM
Russell, H., UN
Russell, J., Crystal Palace
Ryan Series, T.

S & W Kenley Series
S. & W. Series
S. Brothers Series
S.B.Series
S.F.S.(Surrey Flying Services)
S.S. Series
Salmon, J.
Sampson Series
Saunders, A.
Sayer, A.J.
SC & C (Smith, Crotch & Co.)
Scientific Press Ltd., The, London
Scott's Series
Shaw, High Street, Kenley
Shaw's Series, London
Sheltie
Shirley Library
Shirley News Series
Shirley Series
Simmons
Simmons Series
Simmons, J.
Simmons, J.H.
Skilton, Charles
Smith & Co.
Smith Bros., Croydon
Smith, F.M. & Co., Croydon, Kenley & Brighton
Smith, G.
Smith, W.H. & Son
Sormans, Charles
South Norwood Series, The
Spiers, R., Brixton
Stackemann, W. & Co., Teddington
Stanbridge Photo
Stengel
Stevens, S., UN
Stewart & Woolf
Stokes Series
Sweetman, E.A. & Sons Ltd., Tunbridge Wells
Symes, S., TH

TALBA Photographic Co.
Tardrew E.S.
Taylor, A.& G., "Reality" Series
Taylor, H.
Tourists' Association, Turnham Green
Tromp, J.H., Kenley
Tuck, Raphael & Sons. Ltd.
Tudor Library, Selsdon
Turner Bros., Sandpit Farm

UNEEDA Penny Bazaar
Unique Photo Co., Catford
USA Studios

Valentine & Sons Ltd.

W, British Made
W.E.D Series
W.T.W., Croydon
Walker Bros. Series
Walker, Adam & Co.
Walker, John & Co. Ltd., London
Ward, H.
Watson's Series
Weston, P.G.
White, Geo., UN
White, S., Brighton Road
Willard, A.A., Lewisham High Road
Williams, W.H.
Wilson's Big Variety Series
Wilson's Photo Series
Woodland, J.
Wrench Series, Maison d'Art, Croydon
Wyatt, A., High Street, Croydon

Zambra, E.

KEY: NOR = Norbury, SN = South Norwood, TH = Thomton Heath, UN = Upper Norwood

Echo Printing Works, South End around 1910

The Croydon Echo newspaper had been published briefly in the late 1890s in Wandle Road, but this building was in South End, just South of Coombe Road. Smith, Crotch & Co published various local newspapers as prominent lettering on the front: of the building shows. The firm was also an advertising contractor and produced the S.C.& C Series of local real photographic postcards. The building was severely damaged by fire in 1910. It was later used by Messrs Ebbutt as a furniture depository. Although it was a listed building with some particularly fine brickwork, it was demolished in the 1980s and replaced a by a far less distinguished structure. Publisher not known but presumably S.C & C.

C.H.Vicker's shop - 37 South End, Croydon - about 1910

An enlargement of part of a postcard of a typical local shop of the period selling newspapers, magazines, confectionery and postcards. For many years photographs could be printed with postcard backings so this may have been produced in a very small quantity for family use. The gentleman standing at the door is presumably Mr Vickers.

Heavy horses at work - Shirley Schools about 1908

This is an enlarged part of a postcard showing the view from the staff house kitchen looking north across the school farm, towards the Norwood Hills. Several men are hard at work with their horses. The Crystal Palace can be seen in the distance. Publisher not known but thought to be Shirley Schools.

Purley, near Croydon about 1902

The top card is an example of an undivided back postcard where the message had to be written on the same side as the illustration. It shows the Tram Terminus at Purley looking south, before a shopping parade replaced the houses on the right around 1903. The building beyond on the right was demolished only a few years ago, whilst those on the left are still there in 2010. Note reverse writing of message.

The lower card uses the same photograph but it has been 'doctored' to show a night time scene. It has also been produced using the whole photograph covering the space where the message was in the top card. Cards published by F.Frith & Co.

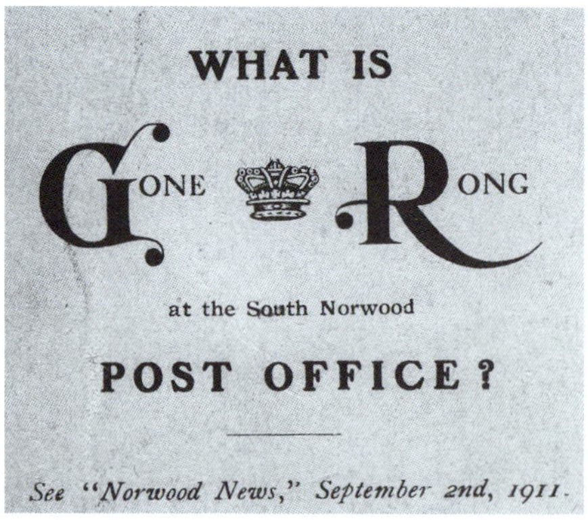

South Norwood Post Off-ish, 1911

This amusing postcard was published in connection with a local campaign to improve the opening hours at South Norwood Post Office. An article in the Norwood News was headed "Closed at Curfew, 25,000 Inhabitants Stamp-Starved After 8 O'Clock pm." Whether it was successful it has not been possible to ascertain but it would be interesting to know what the local residents might make of the situation now, one hundred years later.

Examples of 'doctored' or posed postcards

There is a commonly held view that "The camera cannot lie". However the evidence from a number of postcards proves that some images have been doctored or posed and a few examples are illustrated here. The card of High Street, Croydon is a C.H.Price card of about 1913. The newspaper placard advertises Cody's Flight Result. Sadly the famous aviator was killed in 1913 and C.H.Price must have decided to continue using the photograph with a handwritten amendment to the newspaper placard reading 'Latest Cricket Result', as shown alongside.

The postcard above of Station Road, West Croydon and the small part of a postcard of North End, Croydon both by C.H.Price, show how he has blanked out the shop names of a rival photographer!

On the right are small but enlarged parts of four Norbury postcards from about 1909. From left to right they show Fairview Road, Norbury Court Road, Norbury Gardens and Beatrice Avenue. The same man appears on each card and several others. He may well have been the photographer's assistant employed to carry his heavy equipment but also used to add life to a quiet scene. Published by Batchelder Brothers.

North End, Croydon about 1920

This is the view looking north from a point just north of the Whitgift Hospital. On the left is Wilson's Cafe (see page 15). The adjacent North End Hall was the home of The North End Brotherhood (see page 65). It was purchased by Croydon Corporation in the early 1940s and became The Civic Hall. On the opening of Fairfield Halls in 1962 it closed and was demolished. Beyond is Kennard's department store (see page 83), the site now being occupied by Debenham's. On the right is The Scala Cinema which was later incorporated in the rebuilt Allder's store (see page 91).

This postcard is one of C. H. Price's splendid real photographic cards. It is thought he produced at least 3,000 different views in total, including numerous event cards. For further details see page 6.

The card is reproduced actual size but an enlargement of the lefthand side is below left and of the right hand side is on the right. This demonstrates the immense amount of detail that can be found on real photographic cards produced from glass-plate negatives. The examination of such cards with a magnifying glass is recommended as they contain so much detail that is easily overlooked.

At the foot of the page is part of a postcard written by the photographer.

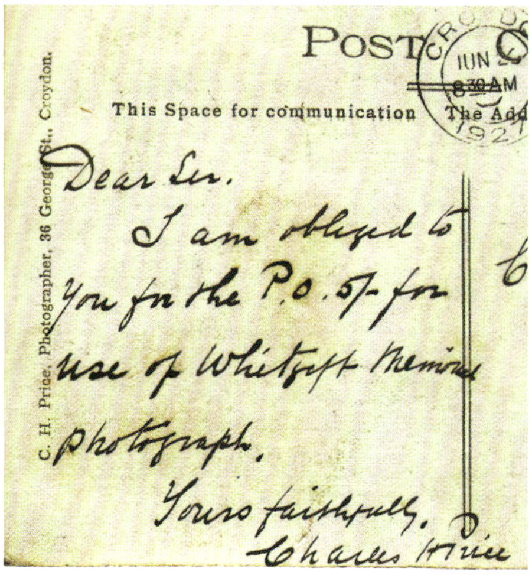
POST C
C. H. Price, Photographer, 36 George St., Croydon.
This Space for communication
Dear Sir,
I am obliged to you for the P.O. 5/- for use of Whitgift Memorial photograph.
Yours faithfully,
Charles Price

W. KING
BY-6182
20014E

1901 TO 1914 EDWARDIAN

No. 15. ADDISCOMBE COLLEGE.

The College at which Lord Roberts received his Military Training.

Addiscombe College about 1809

From 1809 to 1859 this was a military training college belonging to the East India Company. Previously it was regarded as one of the finest country houses in Surrey. In 1861 the college and estate was sold and developed for housing, much of which is now a conservation area. This is a good example of an early postcard reproducing an old view. Published by H.R.Grubb.

Plaiting the Maypole, by Girls from Ingram Rd. Schools, at Croydon Band of Hope Union Fete.

[Photo by B. T. Luckett, 221, Holmesdale Road.

Maypole Dance, June 30th 1906

The celebration of May Day was a regular feature of life in schools until the mid 20th century, usually with dancing around a maypole. Published by B.T.Luckett.

Haling Down Estate about 1908

This is an early example of an advertising postcard with the space for a written message occupied by the printed advert. The houses, mostly still there but without the wooden features, are on the west side of Brighton Road between the crescent arms of Churchill Road.

HALING DOWN ESTATE, PURLEY OAKS.

Rents, £42 per ann. Price—Leasehold, £490; 99 years; Ground Rent, £7 7s. Freehold, £680.
MESSRS. E. H. STODART & CO., on the Estate; or 419, Brighton Road, opposite the Estate;
Tel. No. 1576 Holborn. *or at their Head Office:* 124, Chancery Lane, London.

THIS SPACE MAY BE USED FOR PRINTED OR WRITTEN MATTER FOR INLAND USE ONLY.

THESE CHARMING AND CONVENIENT

SEMI-DETACHED HOUSES

To be LET or SOLD

(Freehold or Leasehold).

These Houses are thoroughly well-built and beautifully fitted and decorated with all modern improvements and electric light.

Situate close to Station and within few minutes electric tram ride of the popular town of Croydon.

THE ACCOMMODATION IS AS FOLLOWS:

GROUND FLOOR—Porch, large Hall, Dining Room and Drawing Room leading into nice Garden. The Domestic Offices are well shut off from the other part of the house, and consist of small Hall with side entrance, capital Kitchen, Scullery, Larder and Pantry, Coal Cupboard and usual offices.

ON FIRST FLOOR—Four good Bedrooms and a Dressing Room, large Bathroom with bath and lavatory (h. & c.) and linen cupboard, usual offices.

In the rear is a nice Garden

with entrance from 10ft. road, convenient for those keeping bicycles, mail carts, etc. There is also Trades' Entrance to each house.

The Houses are built in pairs, alternately with balconies to the first floor.

"The Kozy." Wilson's Oriental Café, 7, North End, Croydon.

Tea Blending, Cutting, and Equalising Machinery.
"The Croydon Tea Warehouse," 7, North End.

Wilson's Café, North End about 1908 (above and left)

The firm of W. E. Wilson was established around 1884 and by the Edwardian period had several shops and cafés in the district. For many years their coffee roasting machine in the window of the North End premises wafted a lovely aroma into the busy street (see also page 12). Around 1960 their North End premises were demolished and they moved the shop and café into George Street before closing in the 1970s. Presumably published by Wilson's, probably for advertising purposes.

South Norwood Railway Hotel about 1904

The Railway Hotel is in Station Road opposite the main entrance to Norwood Junction station. George Amer was Landlord from 1886-1906. The gates on the left-hand side led to railway property. The building remains but the top storey was destroyed by fire in the 1960s. Presumably published by G. Amer.

First Arrival of the New GPO Motor Van at Croydon 1905

A small group of interested spectators watch the new motor van outside Croydon Head Post Office in the High Street in about 1905. One hundred years later this is still the main post office in the town. Early motor vehicles were notoriously unreliable and breakdowns were common (see card at bottom of page 34). The First World War saw great improvements in their reliability and by the early 1920s horse-drawn vehicles began to be superceded. Post card from The R&C Series (Roffey & Clark).

Mitcham Road Peppermint Distillery

The area to the west and south-west of Croydon, including Mitcham and Carshalton, was famous in Edwardian days for lavender and herb growing. Apparently the soil and climate were particularly favourable but the industry largely died out here after the First World War. There has however been a welcome recent revival on a small scale near Woodmansterne.

The Mitcham Road Steam Distillery was just on the Mitcham side of the main entrance to Croydon Cemetery but closed in 1949. The vehicle appears to be an early battery-electric lorry. The firm of John Jakson & Co was French and this card was printed in France.

JOHN JAKSON & C°, Mitcham Road Distilleries, Croydon (England)

Carting John Jakson & C°'s Peppermint Crop to Distillery

RIDDLESDOWN: THE ROSE AND CROWN.

Riddlesdown, The Rose and Crown

This view shows the main London to Eastbourne Road south of Purley. The horse-drawn vehicle seems to be a passenger brake and it may well have brought a small party to enjoy the delights of Riddlesdown on the left followed by the pleasures of the public house on the right. The Rose & Crown was virtually destroyed by a flying bomb in 1944 but was rebuilt after the war. Like so many pubs it has now closed and been replaced by flats. Published in H.R.Grubb's Purley and Caterham Series.

Pages 17 to 32 illustrate a selection of printed coloured cards. Most of these would have been printed in Germany but many were published by local Croydon area concerns. The views are arranged as a geographical tour around the County Borough of Croydon and the adjacent southern districts which later in 1965 were absorbed into the present London Borough. We commence in the town centre with three views that would have been very familiar to the Edwardians.

Croydon Parish Church about 1902

The Parish Church of St John the Baptist in Old Town was almost completely destroyed by a disastrous fire in 1867. The original 14th century tower survived and the church was rebuilt on a slightly larger scale within a few years. Six archbishops of Canterbury are buried in the church, including Croydon's greatest benefactor, John Whitgift. The pinnacles on the main building were mostly removed in the 1960s. Card published by Valentines.

The Town Hall about 1904 (below left)

This is Croydon's third Town Hall, opened in 1896, seen from High Street. The first was more of a market hall built near the High Street in the 16th century and replaced by a Georgian structure in 1809. The third in Katharine Street was built on the site of the Central Croydon station which closed in 1890. The extended building is now known as The Clocktower and includes a new library and museum. Card published by Charles Martin.

The Grand Theatre about 1903 (below right)

The Grand Theatre and Opera House was on the east side of High Street near the present flyover. It was a lovely Victorian Theatre but closed in 1959 to be replaced by a modern but undistinguished office block. Card published by London View Co.

Crystal Palace about 1906

The Crystal Palace was first erected in Hyde Park to house The Great Exhibition of 1851. It was taken down and re-erected here on an enlarged basis in 1854. The building and park were just beyond the Croydon boundary which met those of Camberwell, Lambeth and Penge in the middle of the road junction shown here and occupied by the ornate lampost. For centuries this had been the site of a famous boundary tree, The Vicar's Oak.

The coming of the Palace to this hitherto densely-wooded area made it very fashionable and encouraged a great deal of high-class housing development as many people wanted to live near the Palace with its many attractions. (see also illustration on page 41). Published by Stengel.

Westow Street, Upper Norwood about 1905

A high-class shopping area soon developed to serve the new residents and visitors. Gaydon's shop opened in 1865 on the right) is a good example. The last owner, Frank Gaydon, was a neighbour of the editor of this publication, and told him that it was quite common to get an order for £100 for Christmas presents from one of the big local houses in 1900. It was a great deal of money, and would equate to something like £3,500 today. Published by H.A & Co.

Church Road and The White Hart about 1905

The public house was formerly a low wooden structure but was rebuilt on a much grander scale by the Victorians. With the exception of the church on the left, the buildings seen here have changed little in 100 years. Published by H.A & Co.

Westwood, Upper Norwood about 1900

Many large houses were built in spacious grounds for the wealthy new residents of the area who wanted to live near The Crystal Palace. Westwood was built on Beulah Hill around 1874. It was for many years from about 1880-1892 the home of the famous preacher, Rev Charles Haddon Spurgeon, but was demolished in the early 1930s. Published by Stengel.

The King William the Fourth, Norbury about 1906

This local landmark was just a few yards north of the Croydon boundary but local residents benefited because London licencing laws permitted longer opening hours than Croydon! A splendid steam wagon and several horse-drawn vehicles are standing nearby, the drivers no doubt refreshing themselves in the public house on a summer day. The public house was demolished a few years ago and replaced by flats. Published by Stengel.

London Road, Norbury about 1906

The new electric tramway opened in 1901 and linked the borough boundary at Norbury with that at Purley. There were few buildings at Norbury until the beginning of the 20th century but a flourishing local shopping parade had developed by the time this photograph was taken. The view is looking north with the railway station behind the shops on the right. Published in Field's Surrey Series.

Ederline Avenue, Norbury about 1903

This peaceful rural scene in Norbury is a reminder of the large amount of open country still separating Croydon from London in the Edwardian period. Ederline Avenue was laid out around 1904 and houses had been built on the surrounding land by 1910. Published by W.A. Poole.

Old Farm, Norbury about 1910

Norbury Farm was one of Croydon's original manor houses. Pressures for building in the area included one of Croydon's first council housing estates on this land. The old farm buildings were demolished in 1914 and building started after the First World War. Published in Field's Surrey Series.

Thornton Heath High Street about 1905

The area around Thornton Heath station was developed after the railway came in 1862 and was at first known as New Thornton Heath. The original settlement was a mile to the west around the pond. By the late 19th century a flourishing local shopping centre had grown up as seen here, looking towards the clock tower. Published in The British Mirror Series.

The Pond, Thornton Heath about 1905

This was a well-known local landmark just over a mile north of Croydon town centre. London Road is on the left and the view is looking south. The pond was filled in and a small garden created in the 1950s but the area is still known as Thornton Heath Pond. Published in The British Mirror Series.

Beulah Road Schools, Thornton Heath about 1905

This school was opened as a result of the passing of the 1870 Education Act to serve the growing population of New Thornton Heath. The site is still in educational use, but the building was replaced in the 1930s. Published by B.S.S. Thornton Heath.

Stanley Hall, South Norwood about 1906

The Stanley Halls at the bottom of South Norwood Hill were designed and built at the expense of local benefactor, William Ford Stanley. He lived in a large house, Cumberlow, behind the hall. Adjacent was the Stanley Technical Trades School, a fine early example of a school teaching trades. This rather quirky building is virtually unchanged and still in use. South Norwood Clock Tower at the junction of Station Road and High Street was erected by the grateful inhabitants of South Norwood in recognition of his generosity. Published in Field's Surrey Series.

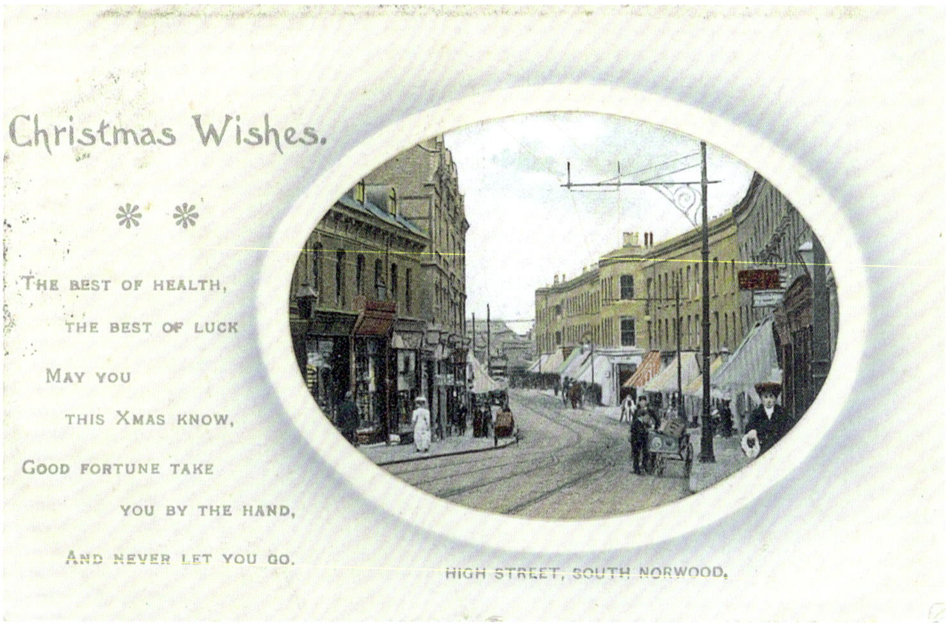

High Street, South Norwood about 1906

It was quite common for postcards to be used as Christmas or Birthday cards as seen here. The local High Street had developed as a shopping street in the 1880s and this view is looking east from the corner of Station Road by the Clock Tower. The view in 2011 is little changed. Published in the Popular Series.

Croydon Common Football Club and Ground, Selhurst about 1907

Croydon Common Football Club's ground was situated on the south side of Selhurst Road near the station. The site is now part of the Selhurst railway depot. The club flourished through the Edwardian period and was nicknamed 'the Robins' a name coined by the press after their claret coloured shirts. Inevitably the ground was known as 'The Nest'. When The Crystal Palace Football Club left the Palace it moved here until taking over its present ground at Selhurst Park in 1924. Published in Field's Surrey Series.

Woodside Green about 1906

Woodside village is about one mile from the centre of South Norwood and retains much of its old atmosphere with its large green. A wagon laden with hay would no doubt have been quite a common sight a hundred years ago. Published in Field's Surrey Series.

The Parade, Woodside S.E. about 1909

Although part of Croydon, Woodside, South and Upper Norwood and Norbury were and are in the London Postal area, which gave them a slightly better postal service. The woman wearing the white apron is outside one of the local hostelries, The Beehive. Published by Clayton & Sons, Stationers, Woodside Green.

Addiscombe Station, Croydon about 1906

The station was opened in 1864 by the South Eastern Railway Company as the terminus on its extended Mid-Kent Railway. The company really wanted to extend the line to Croydon town centre but in the event this was as far as it got. The station closed in 1997 as part of the new Tramlink project and was demolished a few years later. Published in Pritchard's Croydon & County Series.

Lower Addiscombe Road, Croydon about 1904

A rural scene with Bingham Road on the right. The tramway opened in 1902 and shopping parades soon appeared on both sides of the road. The railway bridge beyond the tram terminus carries the Woodside & South Croydon Railway. This was jointly operated by the South Eastern and Brighton companies. It was electrified in 1935. A station was provided in Bingham Road but the line closed in 1983. This section became part of the route of Croydon Tramlink from 1997 and the trams cross the road at street level. A new stop called Addiscombe is situated between Lower Addiscombe and Bingham Roads. Published in Pritchard's Croydon & County Series.

Royal Parade, Croydon about 1907

This is London Road at Broad Green looking south. St. James's Road is on the left. Most of the buildings seen here are still recognisable despite the passing of a hundred years. Published in the British Mirror Series.

Crown Hill, Croydon about 1906

Looking up Crown Hill, Surrey Street is on the right with its street crossing paved with setts. Most street corners had these in Victorian and Edwardian times, especially where roads were otherwise unmade, and a few still remain. Crossing sweepers were employed to sweep them on a regular basis. The Theatre Royal on the left was approximately on the site of Croydon's first theatre. The building seen here became a cinema and eventually closed in 1956. Publisher not known.

George Street, Croydon about 1906

Looking west, the Addiscombe tram is passing Dingwall Road on the right. All of the buildings on the left and most of those on the right were demolished in the 1960s and the road was widened. The building with the tower was Thrift's Grocery Warehouse and the clock came from the second town hall, demolished in 1893. Published in The British Mirror Series.

North End, Croydon about 1904

Looking north along North End, the tram is outside Allder's store which would later be rebuilt and much enlarged. The Whitgift Hospital, right, dating from 1596 is on the corner of George Street and the Crown Hotel, left, is on the corner of Crown Hill. Publisher not known.

Croydon, The High Street about 1898

The High Street had only recently been widened on the left when this photograph was taken. The horse trams were extended through this section which was originally too narrow but it would only be a few years before new tracks would be laid for the electric trams of 1901. Electric lighting had just been introduced in parts of the town and one of the new lighting standards is on the left. Ashby's shop on the right was a fine 17th century building, originally The Red Lion. It was demolished in the 1920s. Published in Misch & Stock's 'Camera Graphs' Series.

High Street, Croydon about 1904

There were still some attractive buildings and shops here at this time. Looking south, The Grand Theatre & Opera House is on the left and beyond in the distance are the brewery buildings of Messrs Nalder and Collyer. Published by A.Wyatt, 103 High Street.

Old Town, Croydon about 1906

This area was known as Le Eldetoun in the thirteenth century. It seems that being low-lying and prone to flooding the main centre of the town had moved early to the higher ground, now High Street. Wooden cottages as seen here were common when local materials were invariably used for building purposes. This area was cleared in the 1930s and Old Town is now a dual carriageway. Published by The London View Co. Ltd.

Waddon Mills, Croydon about 1905

This was the last remaining water mill in Croydon and it continued to grind corn until 1928. This view is looking east towards Croydon. The river here is now much narrower, the water table having been lowered as more water is abstracted and much of the area is built up and less water percolates into the ground. Publisher not known.

Purley from Sanderstead Road about 1906

This view of open downland shows the embankment of the Oxted railway line beyond the fence and past that is the main Brighton line at Putney Oaks. The white cliff is the chalk pit at Haling Lime Works. Virtually the whole area is now covered by housing. Published in Field's Surrey Series.

Church Walk, Addington Park, Croydon about 1908

Addington village and church are situated about three miles south-east of Croydon town centre, and remained remote until the 1930s. The church was much altered by the Victorians. Addington House was largely built in 1780 and the grounds are partly attributed to 'Capability Brown'. From 1808 to 1896 the building, by now Addington Palace, was used by the archbishops of Canterbury as a country retreat. Five of them are buried in the churchyard, and the building was for some years home to The Royal School of Church Music. It now hosts various functions. Published in Field's Surrey Series.

Addington Road, Croydon about 1906

The parish of Sanderstead lies between Addington and Coulsdon and the settlement is at a height of 570 feet (174 metres) above sea level. The present church dates from the 13th century and this view is looking west along Addington Road towards the top of Sanderstead Hill. Published in Field's Surrey Series.

Coulsdon Church, near Croydon about 1907

The settlement of Coulsdon is high on the Downs at about 600 feet (183 metres) above sea level. This area has since the 1920s been known as Old Coulsdon whilst the area in the Brighton Road now known as Coulsdon was formerly Smitham. The church replaced a Saxon building around 1250 and was greatly enlarged in the late 1950s. Published in Field's Surrey Series.

Godstone Road, Purley about 1903

This view is looking south from a spot nearly opposite the present Purley Hospital. The road still divides here with a few trees in the centre but apart from some houses on the right the outlook was almost completely rural. The appalling state of the road was not uncommon at this time. Publisher not known.

Purley near Croydon about 1904

The Queen Victoria Memorial Fountain on the left was unveiled by The Duchess of Albany in 1904. It has since been moved on several occasions and is now outside the library. The chalk cliff is behind Purley Station and the waterworks were behind the railings on the right. This area is now part of a gyratory road system with Tesco on the waterworks site. Published in Field's Croydon Series.

Riddlesdown Road and Viaduct, Whyteleafe about 1908

This could more correctly be called Kenley. The viaduct is the only one in Croydon and was built to span the lime works and chalk quarry. The Croydon & Oxted Joint Railway was a Brighton and South Eastern companies venture, opened in 1884 and it was only electrified as recently as 1987. Published in Field's Surrey Series.

Panoramic View of Purley about 1902

Panoramic postcards are not very common and were subject to one penny postage rate. It would also need one half being stuck to the other somehow or to be sent in an envelope. Russell Hill is on the right with the station in the foreground. There was still a great deal of open downland on the left towards Coulsdon. Published in The Canon Series by M&W. London.

Coulsdon, Brighton Road & Asylum Entrance about 1902

The lodge of Cane Hill Asylum is on the left. The asylum closed in the 1970s. This view is looking north with Brighton Road straight ahead and Lion Green Road to the left. The open downland in the background would be covered by new houses in the next few years. This area was known as Smitham Bottom, the ancient settlement of Coulsdon being some 500 feet (152 metres) high on the Downs about 1½ miles to the east. The card already names the area as Coulsdon but the station opened in 1899 was and is called Smitham, but is to be renamed Coulsdon Town from 2011. Published by F.Frith & Co.

Smitham Downs about 1906

It is difficult to locate this scene as most of it shows bare chalk downland. A few houses in the distance are surveyed by a loan horse rider while the haystack on the left is a reminder of past farming practices. Published in Field's Surrey Series.

The Smithy, Woodcote about 1904

The caption on this card is barely readable. The Woodcote area to the south-west of Purley was developed by William Webb who purchased a large area of land and planted it with hedges and trees so that they could mature before any development started. He provided a village green with stocks and adjacent Temperance Pub, The Lord Roberts, and smithy as seen here. It was still the age of the horse and there were many such establishments at this time. One still exists in the area at Addington. Published in Field's Surrey Series.

Follett's Shop in the early 1900s

As printed above the shopfront, this establishment was at 302 London Road, Croydon. This is unusual in being a coloured view of a shop. Follett's were in London Road from about 1897 until 1909. Presumably published by the shop proprietor.

Early Charabanc about 1919

This advertising card shows an early charabanc with solid tyres posed in a rural location. Vivian Thomas, describing himself as a Motor Job Master, had premises at 110 Canterbury Road from around 1910 until 1929. Presumably published by Vivian Thomas.

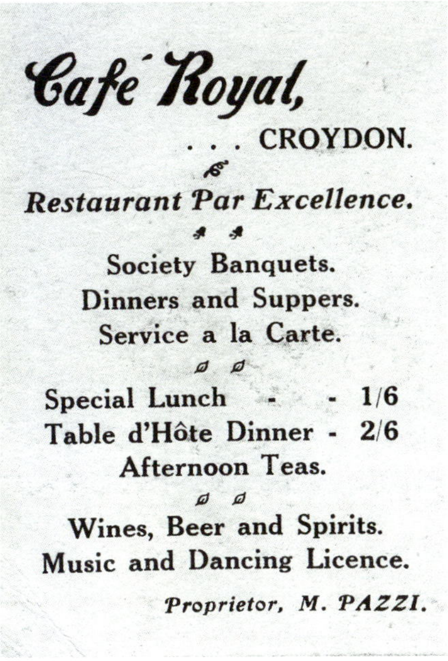

Café Royal Banqueting Hall, Croydon around 1906

The Café Royal was at 80 North End from around 1891 until the mid 1950s. It was opened by Geroni and Pazzi, but from 1901 it was owned by the Pazzi family. It was a popular high class restaurant with a uniformed doorman who generally stood outside to welcome customers and open the door for them. Note the prices. Advertising card presumably published by the Pazzi family.

The Skating Rink, Croydon about 1910

An advertising card for the local Skating Rink. This was in premises in Cherry Orchard Road near the corner of Addiscombe Road from about 1909 until 1915. There was a great, but short-lived craze for roller-skating throughout the country at this time. The building was for many years afterwards occupied by Creed's Teleprinter factory but was demolished in the 1960s. Published by Stafford & Co Ltd, Netherfield, Notts.

Humorous Croydon card about 1907

It was common practice for publishers to produce postcards which could be overprinted with the name of a locality. This must have enabled very large sales of any particular subject. Three cards on the next page (32) are in a similar category. Published in the Burlesque Series.

Humorous Purley card about 1910, (left)

This amusing card is of a drawing by Cynicus who produced many such cards. Published by The Cynicus Publishing Co. Ltd., Tayport, Fife.

It is no crime to kiss in Thornton Heath about 1908, (below left)

Another humorous card with place name added. Published by B. B. Series, London.

Many are called but few get up in Croydon about 1910, (below)

Another humorous card with place name added. The message includes "Shall be home about 5.0. pm R.Bridge". Posted in Croydon and sent to Chatham. Published by J.Salmon, Sevenoaks.

Croydon Grove about 1910

This street is off Sumner Road near the Mitcham Road end. Unfortunately it was comprehensively redeveloped in the 1970s as part of a large scale clearance of the area so these attractive Victorian houses no longer exist. Publisher not known.

Nicholson Road, Addiscombe about 1910

Nicholson Road is off Lower Addiscombe Road and the card was only identified by the Estate Agent's advertisement board, looking at maps and a visit. How much more attractive these streets appeared before they were lined by parked cars. Publisher not known.

Harrington Road, South Norwood about 1905

This suburban street contains a variety of houses with several small shops and a local hostelry, The Albert Tavern on the corner of Albert Road, left. Small groups of people and some vehicles enliven the scene on this attractive card. Published by Talba, South Norwood.

A CHILD'S PLEA.

Just think of me for a moment,
A child of the slum and street,
Forced to school in the early morning,
With hardly a crust to eat;
With a slice of bread for dinner,
And water to drink, or tea—
You're cross if I don't do my lessons,
But lessons are hard to me.

I'm often ill clad and so hungry,
Yet there's sums and there's grammar to do;
My body gets all in a quiver,
And my head's always aching too.
So I can't learn the things that I ought to,
However I frame or fret,
For my mind wanders straight from the lessons,
To the meals that I seldom get.

From the "Echo," 25th April 1904.

Croydon Raw Material 1904

Few postcards show the less attractive side of life. There are very few of the poorer districts and the sun is usually shining. This postcard was obviously posed in a studio as can be seen from the background, although the condition of the children seems real enough. It has been much enlarged here. Croydon had a number of slums at this time and plenty of children would have turned up at school without shoes or socks. The space on the back for the message has been used for the verse. Publisher not known.

A Breakdown at South Croydon in 1907

This photograph was taken in the Brighton Road approximately opposite the site of the present Croydon Bus Garage. The Royal Mail vehicle concerned is similar to but not the same as that shown on page 16. Scenes such as this were common in the days before the First World War. This card was posted to Canada on 26 October 1907 and includes the message "i have sent you a Picter Postcard its got love on it i have put a cross on him so you know him (sic)". Publisher not known.

Ironmongers' shop, Thornton Heath about 1910

Scratchley Brothers shop was at 111 Thornton Heath High Street from about 1907 until after the Second World War. There is so much detail in this photograph that it seemed well worthwhile to enlarge it. The owners appear to have had a good sense of humour judging by the rather witty signs. Presumably published by the owners.

The Bourne Water, Coulsdon about 1906

The flooding caused by the Bourne is in Brighton Road next to the Red Lion (now demolished). Coulsdon Library and a pumping station, also demolished, were built on this site which had often flooded. The shop buildings opposite date from the 1880s and housed the businesses of (from left): Mark Powell (fruiterer), Cherry & Mann (The stores), W.E.Eade (draper), Alfred Cottage (plumber and decorator), R.Rignell (butcher) and L.Shortell (watch-maker). Published by W.T.Eade.

Whitehorse Sanitary Laundry Ltd. Van, pre 1918

A fine postcard of an early van illustrating the use of a horse-drawn vehicle designed body on a motorised chassis. The van is a Léon Bollée vehicle. This laundry was at 359-361 Whitehorse Road, Thornton Heath and the van is shown parked to the south of the yard entrance. The firm started around 1898 and by 1919 changed to the White Heather Laundry so the photograph was taken before the First World War. Laundering was big business then and there were some 120 firms listed in the Croydon area in 1910 although many of these were small concerns. The Whitehorse Road premises were later occupied by a manufacturer of shoe heels. After 1941, Jaques, the well-known sports equipment and games firm, was there until recent times but is now at Edenbridge, Kent. Published by Batchelder Bros.

Welford's Surrey Dairies, Brighton Road, South Croydon in the 1920s

Welford's had a large number of branches in the area. This one at 193 Brighton Road, South Croydon opened in the former premises of Hooker's Dairy around 1922, although the firm became part of United Dairies (London) Ltd. by the early 1930s. Here we see the morning line-up of roundsmen with their handcarts together with other staff behind. The method of distributing milk from lidded cans was normal then. Publisher not known.

Band of the Croydon District Postal Musical Society

Bands were very popular in the days when music was not as readily available as it is today. Brass bands date back to the 19th century. They consist of brass and percussion instruments. Some bands expressed local solidarity or like this one, groups in society. The Croydon Postal Office District had a large staff and there were probably plenty of men able to join the band's activities. The photograph was taken at Farthing Downs. Published by W.J.W.

Swan & Sugar Loaf, Croydon about 1908

The 'Swan and Sugar Loaf' public house dates as far back as 1754 although this building was erected in 1896. The earlier one had been in a building that was the property of the Archbishop of Canterbury and this led to the confusion over the name as the archbishop's mitre was transposed into a sugar-loaf and his crook into a swan. In the front are five open-topped double-deck buses operated by the London Road Car Co. Ltd. which used the name 'Union Jack' as a fleet-name. Published by J. R. Robertson.

Horse-drawn engine of the Croydon Fire Brigade, early 1900s

A resplendent team of seven fireman and their horse-drawn appliance in front of the then newly erected fire station at 10-14 Park Lane. This was built at the corner of Park Street to replace the previous one in Katharine Street and opened on 19th December 1905. The horse-drawn appliances were gradually replaced from 1912 by motorised ones so their use ceased from 1914. In 1961 a new main fire station was built at Old Town and the site shown here became part of the land used for the 23 storey Nestlé Group office block. Publisher not known.

Croydon Temperance Silver Prize Band

Silver bands played lacquered and silver-plated instruments which in those days were more costly than brass ones. There was a Croydon United Temperance Council which aimed at creating unity amongst the temperance movement in the area and there were also temperance Friendly Societies. Published by U.S.A. Studios.

Croydon, London Road

A view facing north from the Broad Green junction. Sumner Road is on the left and St. James's Road on the right. When the old houses behind the fence on the left were demolished in 1933, the Savoy cinema was built on the site and opened in 1936, although now recently demolished. The publisher of this card was the French firm of Levy which frequently offered postcards depicting unusual views so it is not surprising that here we can spot a horse drinking from the trough at the entrance to St. James's Road. There is very little traffic apart from a cyclist and horse-drawn and a tram. Published by L. Levy.

A Bit of Old Purley about 1905

The horse-drawn cart is at the junction of Banstead Road and Brighton Road with Purley Fountain and horse trough to the left. Behind the brick pillars and railings on the right was the Purley Pumping Station of the East Surrey Water Company, now Tesco.
In the centre is the weather-boarded Jolly Farmers with Purley railway station behind it outlined by the chalk cliff in Warren Road. Part of the building to the left survives as a jeweller's and the building behind is in High Street. The white gabled building to the right was the Railway Hotel, now replaced by offices. In 1907 the present Jolly Farmers and the adjacent shops (The Exchange) were built. Publisher not known.

View to North from Asgarth, Riddlesdown Road, Purley (Croydon under fog) 1908

Asgarth in Riddlesdown Road, Purley was situated on the high ground above Warren Road. In 1908 it was the home of L.H.K. Clark, a member of the Croydon Natural History & Scientific Society, who produced this view looking north through the fog towards Croydon. He also used a similar view, taken on a clear day, as a Christmas card on which it is just possible to see the Crystal Palace on the skyline. In 1921 Asgarth was lived in by James Edmund Clark, presumably a relative. Published by L.H.K.Clark.

Old Croydon Series, no.8

John Bartlett of 63 North End was probably the main Croydon bookseller and stationer of those times and fortunately sold a series of unusual photographs taken previously. This view is to the south along Market Street and gives a good idea of what this area looked like, a true remnant of olden times. After the 'Croydon Improvement Act, 1890' was passed, the area between High Street, Surrey Street and Crown Hill was largely cleared and rebuilt although Middle Street and Surrey Street remain. Published by J. Bartlett and it is likely that the postcard was produced by C.H. Price on behalf of Bartlett as the typeface resembles that of Price.

Old Croydon Series, no. 2

An unusual photograph of the stone and flint entrance archway to the Old Palace across what is now Old Palace Road. It was demolished in the 1880s so the picture Bartlett used was taken well before the days of photographic postcards. Published by J. Bartlett.

Ebbutt's furniture shop, High Street, Croydon

Alfred C. Ebbutt had shops in the High Street at nos. 43 and 53 together with one for second-hand furniture at no. 70. He classified himself as a cabinet maker, upholsterer and also undertook removals. The firm also later had a furniture depository at South End (see page 9). This postcard gives a good idea of a typical contemporary bedroom with a wardrobe and dressing table and a wash stand with basin and ewer, although the high-back of the small chair must have been unusual to most customers. Publisher not known but probably Ebbutt's.

Coulsdon Post Office about 1908

Mrs Jeffrey stands outside Coulsdon Post Office proudly holding a five shilling postal order - she was the first Coulsdon woman to qualify for the old age pension introduced by Lloyd George in 1908. The post office was housed in Cherry Tree Cottage, Coulsdon Road, near Bradmore Green and Mrs Jeffrey lived at the thatched lodge house on the corner of Grange Park and opposite Bradmore Pond. There is Edwardian advertising for Cadbury's and, behind Mrs Jeffrey, for R.White's hop ale, lemonade, ginger beer and soda water. Published by Barratt's Photo Press, London EC.

Upper Norwood and Crystal Palace

A copy of an original poster of 1900 advertising the advantages of living in that area. It may well have been issued by the railway in an attempt to encourage people to move from central London and travel in regularly. Publisher not known.

Samuel Coleridge-Taylor about 1910

Croydon's most famous composer, he was born in 1875, the son of a Nigerian born doctor. His childhood was in Croydon and he went on to study at the Royal College of Music. He achieved fame with his oratorio 'Hiawatha' which became widely performed. He composed many other works but died in 1912 at his home in St. Leonard's Road perhaps largely through overwork. Publisher not known.

T. Goddard's shop, 166 Cherry Orchard Road, Xmas 1909

The then customary Christmas display of poultry outside T. Goddard & Sons' shop at 164 and 166 Cherry Orchard Road, Croydon, at the Lower Addiscombe Road end near The Leslie Arms public house. This firm traded as dairymen but this shop-front display must have been very eye-catching on the days before Christmas. Publisher not known.

Crystal Palace balloon flight about 1910

The Crystal Palace was a venue for many big events and the launch of balloons was a favourite attraction. On the day, once the timing and weather conditions were acceptable to the aeronauts, the balloon would be released and here a large crowd watches a take-off with the Palace and one of the towers prominent behind. This postcard was posted on 25th August 1910 but it is not possible to pinpoint the actual event as there were a number of such flights in those years. Published by J. Russell & Sons.

Charles Allan, Coal Merchant about 1905

Charles Allan's trade card shows him with his splendid horse-drawn wagon, perhaps the work of a local carriage maker. The decorated horse's harness and the absence of any coal suggest that Mr Allan's photograph may have been taken specially for the card or possibly when he attended an agricultural show. He appears in local directories at 34 Waddon Marsh Lane from 1897 to 1907. Published by Charles Allan.

The Lord Roberts Temperance Inn about 1910

The Lord Roberts Temperance Inn today houses the Woodcote Post Office and Stores but in Edwardian times the attractions included the pond, tea lawns, coffee room, stocks, see-saw, select teas and cold luncheons and suppers. The stocks remain but the pond has given way to the war memorial. William Webb had specified that a post office was the only business permitted on the Webb estate (Woodcote) and the temperance inn was named after Lord Roberts (Frederick Sleigh Roberts 1832-1914) who achieved great renown in the Afghan war, the Indian Mutiny, the Boer War, Abyssinia and Burma. Published by W.T. Jackson.

London Road, Thornton Heath

A great period view with horse-drawn vehicles as the norm but with the electric tram as the forerunner of what would soon change all transport. The open-topped tram is turning into Brigstock Road. The tram depot and tramways Head Office is the prominent building on the right. The Corporation works car is just entering the depot. Two boys can be seen climbing on the back of the 'Surrey' hoping to go some way free of charge, perhaps even to Croydon. Published by S. Symes.

East Croydon Railway Station about 1910

This station was opened in 1841 as Croydon's second station, the one at West Croydon having been opened two years earlier. It was rebuilt in 1894 with three island platforms and has long been the main Croydon railway station, especially so today with its many fast services to London and the south. In this rather sedate picture the only vehicles are the trams, all other activity being on foot. Plans were started in 1982 which resulted in the erection of a new building of glass and steel which opened in 1992. Another postcard is on page 74. There are plans to enlarge the station which is one of the ten busiest in the country. Published by C.H. Price.

London Road, West Croydon about 1908

This photograph was taken from the corner of London Road. The women on the left are crossing Station Road. The Croydon Corporation tram on the left is on its way to Purley and the South Metropolitan Company's tram on the right is at the terminus of the Sutton and Tooting routes in Tamworth Road. Croydon was unique in the London area in having both corporation and company trams. Relationships between the two operators were sometimes strained and the company was never allowed to connect its tracks in Tamworth Road with the tracks in Station Road which served its Crystal Palace and Penge routes. The view is little changed today but the Railway Bell in the centre is now The Arkwrights Wheel. Published by Batchelder Brothers.

Coombe Corner, High Street, Croydon

A view along South End facing north. The New Inn was at no. 2 South End with Upper Coombe Street as it was then on the right. The Grand Theatre and Nalder & Collyer's Brewery is also visible. Publisher not known.

Coombe Lane, Croydon

This postcard shows what was then listed as Upper Coombe Street, facing west and it is obvious why this road had to be widened. The advertisement on the side of a house is for D.T. Robinson, a plumber, who was at no. 8 Waddon Road in the early 1900s. This stretch of road officially became Coombe Road around 1929. Note the old cottages on the left. Published by C4.

A Corner of the Croydon Central Motor Co.'s Works, 1920s

In the early 1900s this firm had been the Central Livery and Bait Stables. It was in Fell Road but Alfred Bullock, the proprietor, must have realised that he could best bend with the winds of change and added motor cars to his business. By 1924 he dropped the equestrian side of things and traded in motor cars only. Being in Fell Road opposite the Town Hall certainly justified the Central name. The garage was on the south side of Mint Walk which in those days connected with Park Lane and this postcard picture gives a fine impression of German Stroewer cars at that time. The garage was swept away in 1964 ready for the construction of Taberner House which was built between 1964 and 1967 and officially opened the following year. Publisher not known but presumably the Central Garage Motor Co.

Staff at Purley Oaks railway station - about 1912

Nine uniformed and three other members of the railway staff belonging to the London, Brighton & South Coast Railway pose for Florence Baxter, a South Croydon photographer. The gentleman seated second from the right with the braided sleeves is no doubt the station master. Purley Oaks Station was built in 1899 to serve the growing district between Purley and South Croydon and lower Sanderstead. The group is outside the signal box. Published by Florence Baxter.

Stoats Nest Station Train Disaster 1910

On 29 January 1910 the Brighton to London Express crashed into the platform at Stoats Nest Station at 3.40pm because of the derailment of the rear portion of the train. William Rose, manager of Hall & Co., was killed on the platform and six passengers from Croydon, London and Brighton also died as well as 30 passengers being injured. Local scouts, playing football on a nearby farm, arrived quickly on the scene with the troop's stretcher and helped to extricate the dead and injured passengers and remove them to the waiting rooms. The boys, all aged between 11 and 14, also helped in obtaining bandages and dressings. Stoats Nest Station later became Coulsdon North and has since been demolished with the site taken by the Coulsdon bypass. Published by W. Gothard, Barnsley.

G. W. Willis, beer and wine merchant's delivery van

George William Willis became the proprietor of an existing beer retailer's shop at 96 Sumner Road in 1909 and continued for many years. He also traded as a wine merchant at 344 Whitehorse Road. In this picture, the alert horse is ready to go on the rounds. Published by A.E. Pierce.

Bramley Bank, Ballards Estate about 1907

This picture was taken after a successful day's shooting at Bramley Bank which was one of the five lodges on the Ballards estate. Ballards was owned by Charles Hermann Goschen, a banker, from 1872. His new mansion in an ornate European style was designed by F.P. Cockerell who began his career as a country-house architect. His grandfather also had connections with Croydon as he designed the second Town Hall in a classical style on the west side of the High Street. After 1920 Ballards was bought by the Russell School but demolished in 1963 to make way for more suitable school buildings. This estate lodge still remains tucked away off Chapel View, South Croydon. The card was posted on 9th December 1907 so was probably a picture taken that year. It illustrates the rural pursuits still common in the area in the early 20th century. Publisher not known.

Harvest Time at Waddon about 1907

Croydon's agricultural past is captured here in an attractive harvest time postcard, perhaps taken at Waddon Court Farm. The seven farm hands all wear hats as they pose with their ladder and pitchforks while they prepare to build a haystack from the stooks seen in the background. There was still a ready market for hay and corn in Edwardian Croydon as well as a large population of working horses. Publisher not known.

Mr. J. J. Parson's Cow, 'Mayflower', Prizewinner, Croydon Horse Show 1908

Mr. Parsons farmed at Addiscombe Dairy Farm, Addiscombe Road and in 1908 won more than just one prize at this show. The official title of the event was the Annual Show of the East Surrey Agricultural Association and it was held at Ashburton House on 10th June. Many horses were entered and around 150 cattle so competition was fierce on what turned out to be a fine day. Competitions and exhibitions were part of the show accompanied by music by a military band. Mr. Parsons also sold dairy products from his shop at 96 George Street and this later became one of Welford's Surrey Dairies shops. The farmhouse still stands, with its date of construction, 1691, shown in the brickwork. Publisher not known.

The Baths, South Norwood

The baths were situated at the Carmichael Road end of Birchanger Road just after the South Norwood Council Schools. They were destroyed by enemy action in the Second World War and have been replaced by swimming baths in Portland Road. Published by H. Peckham.

Panoramic View of Purley about 1905

A fine panoramic view of Purley shows the railway line running left to right and the rooftops of houses in Brighton Road and Ellen Avenue (now Lansdowne Road). The photographer is standing in Grovelands Road near the site of St. Swithun's Church and the junction of Downlands Road. The building in the centre is the engine shed south of Purley Station. Note the fine residences that have appeared on the hillside above Godstone Road. Publisher not known.

Opening Ceremony, Purley Cottage Hospital by Princess Christian - March 31st, 1909

Princess Christian, one of Queen Victoria's daughters, arrived by car at the new cottage hospital, and observed all the flags and bunting at Purley crossroads. It is not certain whether the Princess is shown to the left of centre amidst an enthusiastic crowd that includes several policemen and boy scouts. The hospital was built in Brighton Road next to the Congregational Church (now United Reformed Church) and despite occasional plans for closure or rebuilding continues to serve local patients. Publisher W.Burdekin.

West Croydon Railway Bridge about 1910

Croydon's first railway station opened here in 1839. It was made busier in 1847 when the line to Epsom was opened and again in 1855 by the line to Wimbledon. This picture was taken at a very busy time of day with steam from a passing train and people watching out for carts and trams before crossing the road. This postcard also shows an interesting mixture of hats. West Croydon Station was rebuilt in 1932/3. Publisher not known.

Church Street, Croydon about 1910

At this time, the name Crown Hill was used for the top part of Church Street although the old numbering was maintained for some years. Many cloth-capped men are seen here, some with bicycles. On the right is the Hippodrome Theatre which opened in 1910 replacing the old Theatre Royal. Films were shown as part of the bill but by 1918 its main theatrical days were over. In 1929 it was the first London area cinema (outside London itself) to have a talking picture system. It closed in 1956 and was a leisure complex for a time. It has been demolished now. Published by J. Geary.

Circus elephants in North End 1912

This lovely picture recalls the time when there were often big parades to advertise circuses and fairs. Lord George Sanger's Circus was the reason for this one in 1912. Behind can be seen shops together with buildings which are still recognisable today. The Empire Theatre advertises Marie Lloyd, the famous singer and entertainer, who was beginning to fade somewhat from her peak popularity as she aged and tastes changed. The Empire Theatre had opened in 1906 as a rebuilding of the National Hall/Grand Theatre of Varieties and was a music hall until the 1950s. It became the Eros cinema which closed in 1959 and was demolished although the entrance area is one of the ways in to the Whitgift Centre. Photograph by C. Walker. Publisher not known.

Whitehorse Road, Croydon

A quiet time along the road facing north with little movement to be seen. The road was largely occupied by small shops although there are a few houses on the left-hand side. The most prominent building is the clock-tower of Gillett & Johnston's Bell Foundry, which has now unfortunately been demolished. William Gillett, a clock-maker, started this firm here in 1844 in Union Road. Charles Bland joined in 1854 and Arthur A. Johnston bought a partnership in 1877. The firm became Gillett & Johnston in 1884 and bell founding was added. This became the key to the firm's success especially after a son, Cyril F. Johnston, who had been head boy at Whitgift School, managed to perfect the art of perfect bell tuning and it became a limited company in 1925. The firm had to close in 1957 although a small business retains the name and expertise in South Croydon. Published by Card House.

St. Peter's, Croydon (Bell moulds by Gillett & Johnston) 1912

St. Peter's Church was designed by Sir George Gilbert Scott and consecrated in September 1851. In 1864 a spire was added and this burnt down almost immediately but was rebuilt without delay. Gillett & Johnston had become world-famous and much of their work was for bells and carillons in the U.S.A. and the Commonwealth. Their fine bells and clocks are still to be found in many places in the world. Of course, not all their work was exported and in this 1912 postcard we see preparations for a new ring of bells to be cast for St. Peters Church, St. Peter's Road, Croydon. A cope, the upper mould, is being lowered onto a core before casting. Publisher not known but probably Gillett & Johnston's.

Croydon Lifeboat Day 1908

Lifeboat Days were a major attraction with the aim of raising funds for the lifeboat service and parades were often local highlights. This one was held on 22nd July 1908. The lifeboats from Southend and Eastbourne took part and the tramcars in the town had collecting boxes for contributions from passengers. The image also has a bell connection for it shows the float of Gillett & Johnston's with some bells, which was pulled by strong horses. The scene here is in Cherry Orchard Road with the fence of Brickwood House grounds on the left. Publisher not known.

Whytecliffe Road, Purley about 1905

A charming group of Edwardian girls poses for the photographer in Whytecliffe Road (now Whytecliffe Road South). Each girl appears very fashionably dressed and holds a hoop, a children's craze. Some of the shops on the left-hand side have survived recent redevelopment opposite the entrance to Purley Station. The first shop on the left-hand side was for many years A.G.Wright's builders' ironmongers. Publisher unknown.

Addington Park Estate Race April 1910

The winner of the race around the estate was Williams who completed the course of just under four miles in 23½ minutes. Considering that Spout Hill, Sandrock and Gravel Hills had to be negotiated the times were considered to be good and only two of the 13 runners failed to finish. The estate was owned by Mrs English who witnessed the race and presented the prizes, including a very pretty silver mounted biscuit box for the winner. The line-up appears at The Cricketers public house in Addington where Howard Bullock invited athletes to enter for another race on 2 May. Publisher unknown.

Recreation Ground, Croydon

A busy scene in Park Hill. This opened in 1888 on land which had been part of the old deer park of the archbishops of Canterbury. The Corporation bought it from the Ecclesiastical Commissioners. Being so near the centre of town, it soon became very popular and like most local parks had a bandstand. After 1930 it had the added bonus of having access to the gardens of Coombe Cliff, the former home of Thomas Horniman the tea merchant. A legacy from Victorian days is the attractive water tower of 1867 on a knoll, which was part of the town's first water system and was in use until 1923. Publisher not known.

Bowling Green, Grange Wood Park, Croydon, 1920s

Grange Wood was bought by the Council in 1901. The card was postmarked in 1933 but probably dates from the 1920s. Bowls was a favourite sport for many years and still retains quite a following today although the number of greens has diminished. This one is still in use. Published by C.H. Price.

The Bazaar, Gardner's Pleasure Resort, Riddlesdown about 1911

Delighted youngsters are enjoying a treat at Gardner's pleasure resort in Kenley. A blue plaque on a Godstone Road house, by a bus shelter opposite Little Roke Road, is the only tangible reminder today of the pleasure gardens that existed on the slopes of Riddlesdown between 1892 and 1934. Attractions shown on the postcard include refreshments, tea rooms, monkey house, drinking fountain, cut flowers, postcards and stamps, fancy bazaar and toy stall. In addition there were donkey rides, swing boats, a miniature railway, aviary, museum, curio shops and coconut shies. Published by Batchelder Brothers.

Spencer's Airship arriving in Croydon. 1st May 1908

On Friday 1 May 1908 there was much excitement in Croydon when an airship was unexpectedly seen descending in a field adjoining Bute Road/Factory Lane. The pilot, Henry Spencer, had intended flying from Wandsworth to circle St. Paul's Cathedral but was blown off-course. However when he had to come down here, he was probably used to this sort of thing and it was not long before he had the downed airship packed onto a lorry and sent to the Spencer works at Highbury. Published by P. P. & P. Co.

1914 TO 1918 THE FIRST WORLD WAR

Mobilisation of The Croydon Territorials - August 5 1914 (above right)

A large contingent of Territorials marching out of Croydon Barracks into Mitcham Road on their way to East Croydon Station. Crowds lined the route to watch proceedings. The original barrack building from 1794 is just visible behind the trees top right. This is one of a number of postcards of the event published by Batchelder Brothers.

Croydon Red Cross Procession probably 1915

The Red Cross Days were organised by the Mayoress' Flag Day Committee to raise funds and 28 such days were held throughout the war. This procession, however, was probably one of the several recruitment processions the largest of which was held on 2nd October 1915 when 2,800 sailors and soldiers took part. Published by C.H. Price.

Tram staff of both sexes during WWI.

A fine line-up of staff at Thornton Heath. The women were employed as conductors and on other work hitherto a male preserve as many men were called up to serve in the army. Publisher not known.

Croydon to France, Croydon Ice Co. lorry (top left)

An unusual picture of a fine gesture by a Croydon firm which provided a lorry to carry supplies to the troops in France. This is standing outside a typical continental café. The Croydon & East Surrey District Ice Company operated for many years from 1900 until the 1980s from their premises at 12 Grafton Road, Croydon. Publisher not known, but presumably the company.

The Crescent War Hospital - 1914-1918 (middle left)

Several private and public buildings were adapted for use as military hospitals including six schools. The hospitals started their vital work in 1915 and closed in May 1919. This picture was taken in August 1917 in the gymnasium of the Boys' School at The Crescent which was used as a massage room. Published by C. H. Price.

Addington Palace War Hospital 1914-1918

In a similar way, this was taken over in 1914 by the Red Cross as a hospital for enteric fever and malaria infected servicemen. Published by Addington Co-operative Society.

Humorous, Wartime Food Shortages about 1917

Food shortages really came to the fore late in the First World War and large queues built up at most food shops. Published by Lansdowne studios, Kenley.

Military funeral near St. Edmund's Church

While most servicemen who died were buried in France and Belgium, nevertheless there were some funerals at home because many homecoming wounded troops subsequently died of their injuries. The Pitlake Mission on the west side of Cornwall Road, virtually in Wandle Park, had been renamed St. Edmund's Church by 1905 when it was incorporated with the Parish Church of St. John the Baptist. Published by Dean.

East Croydon & Addiscombe Plotholders 1919

The shortage of food in the First World War led to the idea of using vacant land for food growing. The Croydon Vacant Lands Cultivation Society was formed. This 1919 postcard is an unusual reminder of these events, the forerunner of the 'Dig for Victory' campaign of the Second World War. Designed by Tardrew, Croydon who was probably the publisher.

Founder's Day, 1918

Here we see the boys and staff of Whitgift Middle School well kitted-out for the annual Founder's Day service at the Parish Church. This event commemorates the laying of the foundation stones of the Hospital of the Holy Trinity (the Almshouses) on 22nd March 1596. The Middle School of 1880 was located in the former Poor School buildings of 1858 in Church Road which were demolished in the early 1930s. The day is still observed each year by all the Whitgift Foundation establishments including the Almshouses, the Old Palace School of John Whitgift, Trinity School and Whitgift School when a church service is held followed by a function at the Almshouses for Foundation members, staff, and selected residents and children. Published by C.H. Price.

1919 TC

National Aircraft Factory at Croydon 1918 to 1919

Croydon had an aerodrome from December 1915 for use by the Royal Flying Corps on farmland west of Plough Lane, Waddon. Not far away but nearer Croydon another testing airfield was built which was attached to the National Aircraft Factory no.1.The construction of this factory began in late 1917 on a 240 acre site to meet the enormous demand for wartime aeroplanes. There were two other such factories in England and this one employed over 2,000 men and women. By the time it got into production in 1918 no one was to realise that the war might be over soon but with the armistice in November, this factory was still churning out aeroplanes and still expecting to reach its target of 200 planes a month. Production was run down from January 1919. Publisher not known.

Peace celebrations, Katharine Street 1919

This day of celebration was on 19th July 1919. The actual Armistice Day the previous year had been unexpected but now the authorities had time to stage a proper celebration. Flags were hung a-plenty and nearly all the Croydon bands took part. At 4pm the Last Post was sounded and maroons fired. In the evening 'The Messiah' was performed in the Parish Church. Publisher not known.

Unveiling of War Memorial in Katharine Street 1921

This memorial is seen here at the unveiling ceremony on 3rd October 1921. The overall design was by James Burford, ARIBA, and the sculptured figures were by Paul R. Montford. Publisher not known.

1939

Croydon Aerodrome, Continental Air Port

This postcard shows the terminal buildings at the first Croydon Aerodrome at Plough Lane, Waddon. It was a collection of somewhat temporary structures a few of which were ex-Army huts but it fulfilled the needs of the time well. The little elevated hut was the control tower. Planes often had to cross Plough Lane from hangars on the west side to reach the main airfield. Published by C.H. Price.

Waddon Aerodrome Post Office

This rare postcard shows what must have been a helpful facility for both passengers and employees and appears to have also been a small shop. It was operated by Rohan et Cie., a French firm that was based in Paris. Published by C.H. Price.

Frederick Frank Minchin, pilot

Once it had been formed in 1924, Imperial Airways issued a set of postcards depicting its pilots and this one shows Colonel Frederick Frank Minchin. He had been educated at Eastbourne College and learnt to fly at the Eastbourne Aviation Company's aerodrome in 1913. After a career with the Royal Flying Corps when he was twice awarded the Military Cross, he joined Imperial Airways and whilst there made a number of important test flights. In 1927 he was on an east-west cross-Atlantic attempt as pilot for Princess Loewestein-Wertheim who wished to be the first woman to fly that way but the plane disappeared. Published by Raphael Tuck & Sons. Ltd.

Imperial Airways, passengers about to embark 1924

The airport was still at Plough Lane in 1924 when this plane was photographed with passengers waiting to board. The plane was G-EBCX, a de Havilland DH 34 which had seating for nine passengers and was first registered in December 1922. Imperial Airways bought it from Daimler Airways in 1924 but it crashed later that year on take-off and was dismantled. Note the Lloyd Loom chair thoughtfully provided for the use of passengers. Published by C.H. Price.

Imperial Airways engine overhauling

The new Croydon Airport opened on land to the east of the old one alongside the then Coldharbour Lane, now Purley Way. A busy scene in one of the hangars at the Airport possibly on the new site. Imperial Airways was formed in 1924 and went on to achieve an excellent safety record.
Published by C.H. Price.

Croydon Aerodrome

The new Airport in Purley Way. Here a K.L.M (the Royal Dutch Airline) Fokker VIII plane is on the left and this was registered in 1929. One of the splendid Handley Page HP 42 airliners, G-AAXE Hengist, is on the tarmac and mail is being loaded or unloaded from a van. The HP 42 and similar HP 45 4-engined airliners were comfortable and reliable although rather slow and had a commendable safety record. However this plane which had been first registered in December 1931 was burnt out at Karachi on 31st May 1937. Published by C.H. Price.

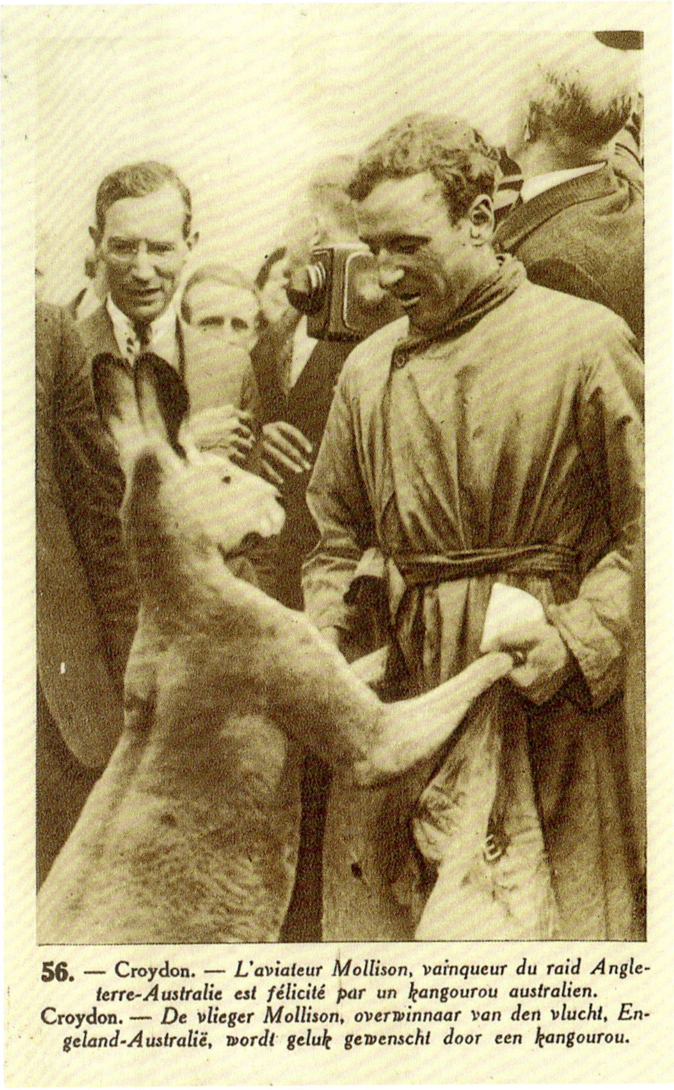

Imperial Airways Air Liner over Croydon Aerodrome

G-AAGX Handley Page HP 42 is flying over the main Airport buildings. The terminal and the apron are on the left with several hangars along the perimeter by Purley Way. The Airport Hotel is just visible on the extreme left. Published by Air Views Ltd.

Croydon - L'aviateur Mollison 1931

Jim Mollison was a Scottish born pilot who made a record flight from Australia to England in July/August 1931 in 8 days 19 hours. He was received at Croydon with acclamation - and by a kangaroo, which was probably not that appropriate as he was not Australian. Mollison was a skilled pilot but rather uncongenial and often the worse for drinking too much. Nevertheless he married an even more famous aviator, Amy Johnson, in 1932 although they divorced in 1938. Published in Brussels, by a Chocolate Company.

Main Booking Hall, Croydon Aerodrome

The postcard shows an empty hall but it was not often like that for it was the hub of Croydon Airport with reception and waiting area, airline offices, a post office and a bookstall. Behind the camera was a meteorological board and through doors, rooms for the other functions that were necessary even in those days for such things as immigration, and the Customs & Excise Hall, and there were also the other airline offices and access to the tarmac. At that time there was an island clock which displayed the time for different parts of the world and this can be seen on the right of this picture. This pioneer building was opened on 30th January 1928 and passengers and goods soon came here from all over the world. It is still there and can be visited on open days, although Croydon Airport closed in 1959. Published by C.H. Price.

Air View of the Convent of the Faithful Virgin, Central Hill, Upper Norwood about 1924

Surrey Flying Services of Croydon Airport specialised in joy-riding flights but also issued a series of interesting aerial view postcards which are now a useful source of what places were like at the time. Here we have a fine aerial view of the Convent in Central Hill, Upper Norwood which came here in 1848 when the Fidelis School was also established. The original building had been a hunting lodge and later was called Norwood House. The surroundings were still positively rural at this time. Published by S.F.S.

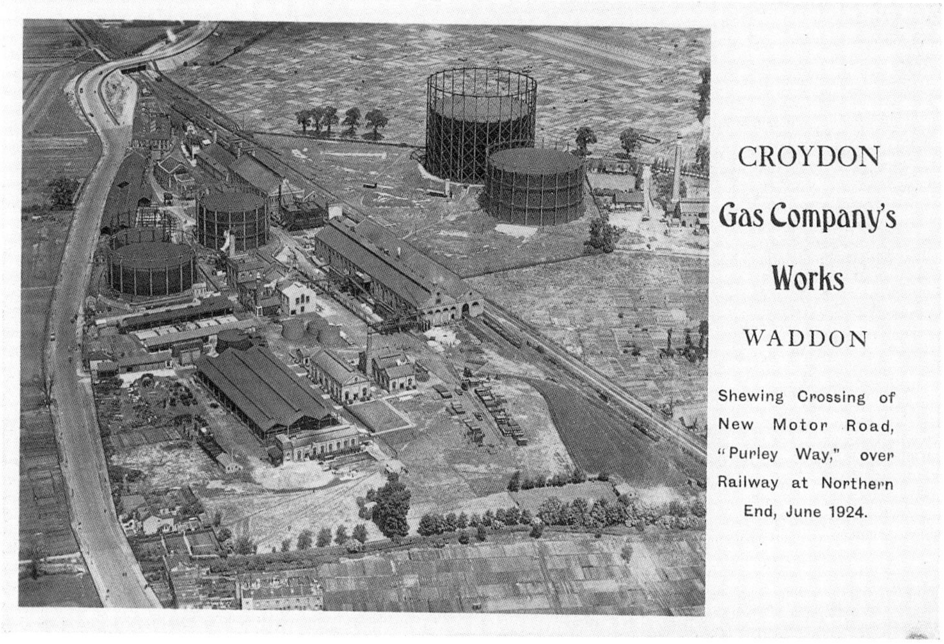

Croydon Gas Company's Works, Waddon

The first Croydon gas works was built in Surrey Street around 1830 and in 1846 the Croydon Commercial Gas & Coke Company took it over. In 1867 a new works was opened at Waddon Marsh Lane on a 42 acre site which had a railway line through the grounds, a big advantage for coal deliveries. The works were extended several times and in the 1920s there were some 5,000 employees. There was also a head office at the east end of Katharine Street which had showrooms and a lecture hall and this was replaced by a stylish new building in 1939 which remains, albeit temporarily empty. In this picture, the road on the left is the New Motor Road which was opened in 1925 as Purley Way. The name Waddon was used to cover a wide area to the west of the centre of Croydon. Published by S.F.S.

Whitgift Grammar School, Croydon, from the Air

The North End buildings had been designed in 1868 in Gothic style and were opened in 1871. The playing-fields stretched as far as Wellesley Road. Passers by could watch the school sports and games through railings. The shops along North End remain but the school was demolished in 1965 after the Whitgift Governors had decided in 1961 to realise the value of the school site having previously bought a new one of some 24 acres at Shirley Park. The new school opened there in 1965 and was officially opened in 1966. The site is now the Whitgift Centre and the entrance area from North End is still visible. Published by S.F.S.

Queen's Road Homes, Queens' Road, Croydon, from the Air

This large building dates from 1866 and was the Croydon Workhouse. There had been a workhouse at Duppas Hill but the increase in population created a need for something much more substantial to provide for the poor. The foundation was laid in 1865 and the building opened on 25th September 1866. During the winter months it often had 2,800 inmates although in summer numbers dropped to about half of that. The number of inmates declined when the responsibility for the poor passed to the Council in 1930 and it was renamed the Queen's Road Homes. In the Second World War it was used as a hospital but badly damaged by bombs in 1941 and 1944. Although much of the building has gone, the central part remains with the tower as a symmetrical building and is being adapted for housing. This part of north Croydon retained quite a lot of open land at this time. Published by S.F.S.

Croydon Corporation Housing Estate. 238 houses. Built by Perry Bros. mid-1920s

Building of this estate had begun in the mid-1920s and the roads were named after Croydon mayors or then prominent officials. Denning Avenue was named after a mayor and this road is that most clearly seen, at an angle from left to top. Published by S.F.S.

The Shirley Schools nr. Croydon, from the Air

The spacious lay-out on an 80 acre site of the Shirley Oaks School buildings was unusual and included a farm as well as a residential home for children. The cottages were named and followed a sequence to make location easier. The school water tower can be seen in the centre distance. The school was closed in 1983, and new houses and flats were built on much of the land. Published by S.F.S.

Standard Steel Co.,Waddon Marsh Lane - about 1925

A multi-view card of the Standard Steel Co. Ltd, structural and mechanical engineers. This is a reminder of Croydon's industrial past. The views show the works and entrance from Waddon Marsh Lane and the foundry and a very busy machine shop. The factory was situated near the Borough Hospital and Progress Way. Following the construction of Purley Way, the name Waddon Marsh Lane disappeared and the company became Standard Steel (1929) Ltd at 72 Purley Way. Published by Standard Steel Co.

Firemen's Medal Day, Katharine Street - 23 October 1920

Several fire engines, tenders, fire escapes and appliances were active in Katharine Street but on this occasion there was no fire. Drills took place opposite the Town Hall on the occasion of Lord Ashcombe, Lord Lieutenant of Surrey, representing King George V, presenting long service decorations and British Empire Medals to Croydon firemen for brave work in World War I, notably on the night of an air raid on Croydon. Councillor Heath Clark was present in scarlet robes as Mayor of Croydon and British Empire Medals were awarded from a carpeted Town Hall entrance to Chief Officer J.W.Dane, Firemen F.W.Botting, A.J.Powell and David Cochrane. The awards were followed by rescue drill, motor pump drill and hydraulic drill and a line of hose played on the gallery above the Town Hall clock. Publisher unknown.

West Croydon Railway Station bridge under reconstruction about 1922

West Croydon Station was opened on 5th June 1839. This was not the first time the London Road bridge needed widening and this work was carried out around 1922. Little doubt that it led to the customary congestion for the general traffic, buses and trams although the postcard does not show this. Publisher not known.

The Red Deer, South Croydon 1924

A fine display of Thomas Tilling's open-top buses dominates this view of the decorative frontage of the Red Deer public house, situated on the corner of Brighton Road and Sanderstead Road. The red deer at the top of the building can clearly be seen and there is advertising for Croydon Ales from Crowley's brewery - one of three large Croydon breweries at this time. Note in the centre of the photograph the bus driver, in his summer uniform, topping up the radiator with water. Publisher not known.

The Terminus, Thornton Heath about 1926

An open-top bus and a tram destined for the Red Deer help to make an animated postcard of Thornton Heath High Street. The photographer is looking west and on his right is The George public house that still displays advertising for Truman, Hanbury and Buxton's London Ales. The single storey building on the left is on the corner of Gillett Road and is today a betting shop. Published by Reval.

Selhurst Park, 1926

The flag of Crystal Palace Football Club flies strongly over Selhurst Park. The view is taken from a house at the junction of Holmesdale Road and Park Road on a match day soon after the Club's move here from The Nest. The first match at Selhurst Park was on Wednesday, 30 August 1924 when Crystal Palace played Sheffield Wednesday while the grandstand, shown here, was still being constructed. The playing area had been levelled prior to football being possible. Crystal Palace F.C. was founded in 1905 and retained an interest in The Nest (near Selhurst Station) when they handed it to Croydon Tramways F.C. Publisher not known.

Mersham Road, Thornton Heath about 1920

View to the north-east. The land on the left was not built on for some years but inevitably used for houses from the early 1930s. The house behind was named 'Beulah' and the postcard was sent by a resident there in 1920. The land seems to be in use for small-holdings. Publisher not known.

Shirley Hills

Silver birches and pines have now encroached on the slopes near Badgers Hole, seen here as part of a small community off Oaks Road, Shirley. Though there is still a settlement here the older houses have disappeared. A well known Croydonian who was born at Badgers Hole in 1870 was W.H. (Peter) Mills. He had a great interest in the area and painted a picture of the Badger Inn, the meeting place for badger baiters in Dunks Hollow, later Badger's Hole. He also sang in the choir at Addington Church and died in 1951. Published by J. J .Dean & Son.

Sanderstead about 1924

Looking towards Briton Hill Farm, a field of corn stooks is an attractive feature of a postcard that shows Sanderstead before it lost its rural charm. The photographer is looking across the site of the present Farm Fields with Sanderstead Hill behind him. The house on the left is No.1 Hook Hill whilst its near neighbour with the external chimney breast is a house called 'steep' on the corner of Hook Hill and Arkwright Road. Both houses today are concealed behind tall hedges. Briton Hill Road has since been constructed behind the line of farm buildings and haystacks. William Stobbart was the last farmer here. Published by W.H.Drake.

North End Brotherhood, North End Hall, Croydon early 1920s

This hall lay between North End and 2 Church Street. There were entrances in both streets. The Brotherhood was formed in January 1912 as a religious movement. Later on the hall was called the North End Hall and then the Civic Hall. It was used for such things as concerts (by, for example, the Croydon Symphony Orchestra) and school prize-givings. It closed in 1962 when Fairfield Halls opened. This postcard dates from the early 1920s. Publisher not known but presumably the North End Brotherhood

Scene of Fire, Oval Road, Good Friday, 1924

At 10.02pm on 18th April, 1924 a serious fire was discovered on the premises of Marlborough Motor Carriage Works (Messrs J. Gurney Nutting & Co.) and the Croydon Wood Heel Co. The efforts of Croydon fire brigade were augmented by firemen from Penge and Sutton but a large block of buildings was burnt out and the flames extended to a large shed where 21 motor cars were housed. Tongues of fire ignited tyres, exploded petrol cans and tanks, and twisted and buckled frameworks. Fireman G.Legge received treatment for injuries but returned to the fire that caused £25,000 - worth of damage. Published by E. S. Tardrew who sent this card to the Superintendant of the Fire Brigade at Park Lane Fire Station offering to supply copies at 2d each, cash with order.

View from Haling Down about 1924

The photographer's view from the chalk cliff at Haling Down shows houses in Biddulph Road, South Croydon in the foreground. Montpelier Road is on the right and Brighton Road runs parallel with the railway line just south of Purley Oaks Station. The fields on this side of the railway were later developed as Braemar Avenue and Grange Road and the untidy site opposite Biddulph Road is currently a Croydon Council refuse and recycling centre near the Royal Oak. The four gabled rooves on the left belonged to The London Electricity Company, but the building was later taken over by, amongst others, the Croydon Advertiser. Published by W.H.Drake.

South Croydon Salvation Army Band 1928

An impressive display of musical instruments is the feature of this postcard of the band of the South Croydon Salvation Army. There is only one lady in a group of 24 musicians that was photographed inside the Salvation Hall, Brighton Road. The hall, though no longer used by the Salvation Army, exists just south of the Whitgift School playing fields between the junctions of Jarvis Road and Newark Road. Its foundation stones were laid on 24th July 1912 by amongst others, Alderman Trumble, Mayor of Croydon. Published by Archie Handford.

High Street, South Norwood about 1925

A view in an easterly direction looking from near the Clock Tower with Portland Road in the distance. This street was developed in the years between 1860 and 1870. A tram can be seen and the number of boater hats is a nice reminder of the times. Publisher not known.

Brighton Road, Coulsdon - about 1928

The Red Lion forecourt is in the foregound of this rainy day view of Brighton Road near its junction with Chipstead Valley Road. A blue liveried East Surrey Traction Company bus is collecting passengers but there is little traffic. Although the shop fronts frequently change, the outline of Coulsdon's shops is remarkably familiar today although redevelopment of the Red Lion site is anxiously awaited. Note the Smitham railway bridge in the distance. Published by Marsh's Library.

CHRISTMAS SNOW. 1927.

OUTLOOK FROM REAR OF 41 DOWNS COURT ROAD, PURLEY, ON 28 12 1927. Photo: J. E. Clark

Outlook from 41 Downs Court Road, Purley 28.12.1927

41 Downs Court Road is situated just above the turning for Cliff End and was originally called Craigellachie. J.E.Clark has captured this snow scene looking north towards Selcroft Road. The Victorian house on the left is No. 15 Selcroft Road, a much older house than its neighbours on the opposite side of the road. The photographer seems to be the same Mr Clark who recorded the view from Asgarth, Riddlesdown Road shown on page 38. Published by J.E.Clark.

Marlpit Lane, Coulsdon - December 1927

An unknown man gives a passable impression of a scarecrow as he indicates the width of a track cut through the snowdrifts on Marlpit Lane in the harsh winter of 1927. Before the construction of houses in the early 1930s the lane was much narrower and the only building was Keeble's Farm, that survives today as No. 22. Old Coulsdon residents were cut off and when the snow melted there was considerable flooding at the foot of Marlpit Lane as seen on the card below. Publisher not known.

Floods in Marlpit Lane - 1928

Traffic and pedestrians carefully negotiate a flooded Marlpit Lane near the entrance to Coulsdon South Station. Although the Bourne flows periodically in an open ditch on the Reddown Road side of the station, floods in this view were caused by the melting of snow after the heavy 1927 snowfall. The area between Marlpit Lane and the Red Lion was regularly flooded until the construction of a pumping station next to the Red Lion. The sign above the railway arch refers to the development of the area in Marlpit Lane, Chaldon Way, Bradmore Way etc. Published by TIC.

The Church and Court, Sanderstead, 1920s

All Saints' Church has a long history but that of the Court is somewhat shorter dating from before 1676. It was initially a two-storey brick building and this was extended to the north with a three-storey block and a wing, the mansion seen here. In 1928 it became the Selsdon Court Hotel which was linked with the Selsdon Park Hotel. A wartime fire here was, in the words of the War Damage Commission, caused by "something dropped from an aeroplane". The owners had the mansion demolished in late 1958. Published by W.H. Drake.

The Glade, Monks Orchard, 1923

This picture shows The Glade, Monks Orchard. The message includes "My land runs right through the wood seen here in the distance. Saw rabbits and pheasants in my part of the wood on Saturday last. Percy." Had Greenview Avenue existed then, it would have been in the far distance on the right-hand side. Much of this area was part of Ham Farm and the house itself occupied the triangular area between The Glade, Elstan Way and Woodmere Avenue. In the 1920s it was bought by Harry Cameron whose professional name was The Great Carmo, an illusionist and circus-owner. He kept a menagerie here which caused some unusual noises and incidents in the area. He had to sell up when his circus tent burnt down in 1935. Published by W.H. Drake.

Wandle Park, Croydon

The River Wandle was a natural water supply to this area but was often blamed for health problems. The Corporation bought land here and laid out the park in 1890. The intention had been to divert the Wandle to run through the lake but it was found best to make it flow in a culvert which avoided fouling. Boating was a popular pastime but in more recent times the lake was filled in although there is now a scheme for re-constructing it. Published by W. H. Drake.

Whitehorse Lane Corner - South Norwood Hill S.E. about 1924

South Norwood Hill was lined by many fine trees when this photograph was taken. A few years later the Norhyrst housing estate would be built on the land to the left of the bus and the Elm Park Estate would be built behind the houses on the right. The house on the corner was later in the 1930s, the surgery of Dr Bell-Nicoll and still houses a doctor's surgery. A small triangle of grass remains but the junction is now extremely busy and is controlled by traffic lights. The route 169 bus was on its way to Wembley. A number of bus routes were extended there for cup finals and during the various exhibitions of the mid 1920s. Published by W.H.Drake.

View from Croham Hurst, Sanderstead

This area of upland of nearly 85 acres was bought by the Council from the Whitgift Foundation in 1901. It was much favoured for the views that were then clearly visible, the top being nearly 500 feet above sea level. It is an eroded chalk hill with sand and pebbles. The area seen here is now almost covered by houses. Published by W.H. Drake.

The Broadway, Selsdon about 1929

A view to the east along Addington Road dating from around 1929 when the open-topped double-decker buses were operated by the London General Omnibus Company before closed tops were fitted. Selsdon started its growth in 1925 as Selsdon Garden Village and the houses then were largely occupied by married couples with children. This estate was built by Costain as were other parts of Selsdon into the 1930s. The block of shops remains largely the same today but the site on the right is a Sainsbury's store, library and hall. Published by W.H. Drake.

Kenley R.A.F. Aerodrome - about 1935

The aeroplane parked outside the hangars is a Bristol Bulldog 11 of No. 17 Squadron. Some of the hangars at Kenley were constructed in 1917 and survived until a fire destroyed them on 23 October, 1978. Prior to their construction the Royal Flying Corps was looking for sites for Aircraft Acceptance Parks which were to be used for assembling and testing aeroplanes destined for squadrons in France. Objections to the site on Kenley Common were swept aside and after World War I Kenley became vital to the air defence of London and played a very significant part in the Battle of Britain and later air operations. Although only a few historic buildings remain the aerodrome is currently used for gliding and recreation. Published by Judges Ltd.

St. Anselm's, Croydon

This pleasant building at 56-58 Park Lane was previously part of the Friends' School and around 1908 became St. Anselm's School, a private one which became well-regarded. Unfortunately perhaps it is now remembered for being blown up in 1940. Land mines were then a real problem and one floated down by parachute near the Town Hall and embedded itself 5 feet down with the rest exposed. A naval squad started attempts to remove it and the area was cleared on 30th September 1940. Alas, the mine (which was very powerful) exploded and down came many houses including St. Anselm's School which was split in two. Published by P. & A. Buchanan.

Coombe Hill House (Ruskin House)

This early 18th century house at 23 Coombe Road, on the corner with Park Lane, was originally a private residence named Coombe Hill House. From the 1930s it was used for a preparatory school but was damaged by bombs in 1944. Repairs were carried out and in 1966 it was bought by the Labour Party to replace the former Ruskin House in Wellesley Road. It is the main venue for the meetings of the Trade Union and Labour Movement in Croydon. Published by P. & A. Buchanan.

St. Anne's College, Sanderstead

This college was built in 1909 as a southern area Catholic school linked with Coloma School in central Croydon. It was extended over the years but closed in 1980. The site is now occupied by housing but the name of the apartment block directly on the school site is 'Theresa's Walk', a reminder of the name, albeit anglicised, of a former headmistress, Mother Thérèse-Marie. Published by Stanbridge.

'Paper Jack', the eccentric Croydon tramp mid-1930s

Frequently seen around the area in the mid-1930s was the mysterious figure known as 'Paper Jack' who wore newspaper for clothing. He slept in fields or in allotments. In fact he was Alfred Ellis Preece who was born in 1876 and had been a surveyor. For reasons not known now, he decided to adopt a new life-style but his tramping around proved fatal on 20th January 1935 when he was run over by a car in Benson Road, Waddon and died before the ambulance reached the General Hospital. Publisher not known.

Limpsfield Road, Sanderstead about 1935

On the right are barns of Borough Farm and the furthest one was used as a garage for some years. The Limpsfield Road was widened early in 1936 so this postcard photograph was taken somewhat earlier. Publisher not known.

Croydon Tramways Company two-horse car, 1898

The three views on this page and that at the top of page 73 are all by O.J.Morris (see publishers details on page 6). This view shows a horse tram on its way to Norwood at The Gloucester, with Whitehorse Road straight ahead and Northcote Road to the right. The Croydon Football Ground was behind the hoardings. Published by O.J.Morris.

Norbury Tram Terminus, 1919

The corporation trams had reached the borough boundary at Norbury in 1901 but it was not until 1908 that the LCC trams were extended from Streatham to meet them and it was 1926 before the tracks were joined and through trams could run from Purley to London. The letter P on the headlight of the corporation tram was introduced to identify the destination, Purley, in the wartime blackout. Published by O.J.Morris.

Coulsdon North, 1929

This view shows an ex-London, Brighton and South Coast Railway overhead electric AC train on the left, with a Southern Railway DC train on the right. When the railway companies were amalgamated into the 'Big Four' in 1923 the Southern Railway decided to adopt the third-rail system which already partially served both former South Eastern and South Western systems. The overhead system on the Brighton lines was therefore abandoned. Published by O.J.Morris.

Waddon Marsh - about 1929

This view is from Purley Way with a train from Wimbledon to West Croydon approaching. This line would very shortly be electrified and several later attempts were made by British Railways to close it. In 1997 it closed for conversion to Tramlink and now enjoys a frequent service and carries far more passengers than ever before. Published by O.J.Morris.

West Croydon Station - about 1930

This view shows the old 1840s station before rebuilding in the 1930s. The terminal part on the left had an overall roof. The newly electrified Wimbledon branch train as seen on the card is standing in its own bay platform. Publisher not known.

Woodside Railway Station - about 1920

A South Eastern and Chatham Railway train has just left the station which was opened in 1871 to serve the nearby Croydon Racecourse after the Addiscombe branch opened in 1864. Even as late as the 1950s small stations often had a minimal freight facility. In 1885 a junction with the Addiscombe branch was formed by The Woodside and South Croydon Railway about 100 yards behind the bridge on which the photographer was standing. Croydon Tramlink now runs along here with new platforms. The old station building on the bridge remains but is boarded up and out of use. Publisher not known.

East Croydon Station and Hall's yard 1937

The tracks and a platform looking north. A steam engine is passing the premises of Hall & Co. which was an important business here. Another postcard showing the main buildings of East Croydon Station is on page 42. Publisher not known.

Hall & Co. Ltd., Croydon 1936

A staff postcard showing a line-up at the Head Office at Victoria Wharf, Cherry Orchard Road by East Croydon Station. The firm was started in 1824 when George Valentine Hall took over a limeworks and stone quarries at Merstham. This was the start of what was eventually one of the largest building material firms in the south-east for, with the advent of the railways, a new site was acquired in 1848 at Croydon in what was then Coney Lane. This later became the Head Office. Growth inevitably led to the need for larger buildings so the original cottages were demolished and in 1930 this fine 3-storey Head Office was opened after designs by Wallis Gilbert & Partners. It remained until the 1970s by which time Hall & Co. had become part of the Ready Mixed Group. Publisher not known.

"The Alexandra Series". Copyright. No. L.2010.

BEULAH SPA HOTEL, UPPER NORWOOD.

Beulah Spa Hotel, Upper Norwood

This large hotel was in Beulah Hill at the top of Spa Hill, Upper Norwood. It was replaced by a new building in 1936. Beulah Spa was once a popular health and pleasure resort with a spring of alleged curative water, enhanced by musical events, dancing, balloon ascents and fireworks. It was a success for some years but once the Crystal Palace was re-erected in the area in 1854 all was lost and it closed in 1858. The 1936 hotel remains as a Harvester Pub and Grill. Published by Talbot, Upper Norwood.

Surrey Street Market, about 1935

A crowded Surrey Street market has been photographed from an upstairs window in Crown Hill. Looking south there is only one modern building to be seen and that is the Davis Theatre in the distant High Street. The stall holders maintain a Croydon tradition going back to 1276 when Archbishop Kilwardby obtained a charter for a market and a fair. The Victory and the Royal Oak public houses were at this end of Surrey Street but have now closed. The Dog and Bull, bearing a date of 1431, remains however but now has competition from The Goose at the southern end. The shops on the left displaying the name J.H. Roff jut out over the pavement, supported on wooden posts. They are clad in mathematical tiles, one of very few examples in the London area. Published by C.H. Price.

Shirley Park Hotel

Originally Shirley House. An earlier building was replaced in 1720 and this was the core of what was to be the hotel later on. It was subsequently enlarged by a banker, John Maberly, who also added to the estate. In 1839 it was bought by John Scott who soon became the second Earl of Eldon. His father had been Lord Chancellor but the second Earl lost his mind and died in sad circumstances at home here in 1854. The house was then often leased and became a hotel in 1914 as Shirley Park Hotel with its own golf course, tennis courts and lake. It was sold in 1959 to the Whitgift Foundation, closed in 1962 and is now the site of Trinity School of John Whitgift. Published by Shirley Series.

Spring Park Farm Estate, Shirley, Croydon

Development in this area had been started before the First World War and continued for many years. At the time of this advertising postcard, houses were on sale for £675 which seems very low but shows how real property prices have increased. Publisher not known but presumably an advertisement by the builders.

ATTRACTIVE SEMI-DETATCHED RESIDENCES COMPRISING ENTRANCE HALL, 2 LARGE RECEPTION ROOMS, BREAKFAST ROOM, SCULLERY, 3 BEDROOMS, TILED BATHROOM (with basin hot and cold), AND CONVENIENTLY PLACED DOMESTIC OFFICES, GOOD GARDEN, GARAGE SPACE, ELECTRIC LIGHT, GAS, MAIN DRAINAGE, ETC., 30 ft. FRONTAGES.

PRICE £675

SPRING PARK FARM ESTATE
SHIRLEY, CROYDON

Telephone : Spring Park 1324 — Estate Office : WEST WAY

SPRING PARK FARM ESTATE. SHIRLEY. CROYDON.

Swimming Pool, Croydon about 1938

The Purley Way swimming pool was a valuable leisure resource situated on the corner of Purley Way and Waddon Way and was opened on 20 July, 1935. The pool was 200ft long and 70ft wide and cost just over £15,600, accommodating 1200 people. Its closure in 1979 was much lamented and it has been replaced by a garden centre using some of the original buildings. Published by C.H.Price.

Thornton Heath Pond about 1936

This was the hub of the London Road end of Thornton Heath and remains so today. The pond itself was filled in during the 1950s but the land remains with traffic swirling round the one-way system. Published by E. Wilson.

Garage at Thornton Heath about 1935

This postcard dates from around 1935-1936 and shows a small line-up of cars for sale including two with open-tops. From the left are a Morris Minor, Ford 8, Wolseley Hornet, Riley Monaco and MG Midget. The firm in 1934 was The Pond Car Mart at 781b London Road, Thornton Heath, a little to the north of the pond. In 1937 it was listed more fully as Jack Feathers, The Pond Car Mart. Publisher not known but probably the Pond Car Mart.

Zeeta, Croydon - Restaurant about 1925

A popular venue for meals, and formal dinners were also held here. The shop in 19-21 George Street was of the customary bakery and confectionery type. The firm had been created in 1919 by some directors of the London department store, Barkers of Kensington (John Barker & Co. Ltd.) and there were a number of shops which also had restaurants. This particular one, which dates from around 1925, had an unusual horizontal tubular glazed window which gave an enhanced view of the products on sale. The firm continued after 1945 but the shops were closed generally in 1958 although this Croydon one kept going until 1960. Photograph by Howard M. King. Publisher not known.

Grant's Roof Garden, showing Dahlia Beds

Grant's was started as a modest drapery business in 1877 by Richard and William Grant from Devon. They already had experience of London stores and based their policy on quality rather than quick turnover. With the big rebuilding scheme for the area west of High Street in the 1890s, a bigger new store was opened in the High Street. It was extended in 1929 and it became the most up-market of the three Croydon department stores. The roof garden was at the top of the new block and offered views of the distant Airport. Published by The Photochrom Company Ltd.

Croham Hurst Golf Club, South Croydon about 1928

The Croham Hurst Golf Club was founded in 1911 and is shortly to celebrate its centenary. The original nine hole course was designed by Fred Hawtree and James Braid (five times Open Champion). It was Braid who officially opened the club by teeing off in 1912. This temporary course was in use for a few years, but the present, larger course was in use by 1910. The view of the interior of the Clubhouse shows the popularity of Lloyd Loom chairs and polished tables. Published by C.H.Price.

Bridge Place, Croydon

This small road was tucked away beneath Windmill Bridge, St. James's Road. Nearby was A. Mason & Co. at 205-207 St. James's Road, a printing firm, which also published greetings cards and postcards. These houses were swept away after the Second World War and replaced by other housing. Published by Denby Series.

Lodge Lane, Addington in the 1930s

Sales of this postcard must have been small for there were then few houses in the new part of Addington. The First National Housing Trust started with some smallish but well-built houses along what was part of Lodge Lane, later Parkway. This extended to the land between here and Salcot Crescent, Gascoigne Road and Wolsey Crescent. They were originally rented and there were also a few shops. The Second World War stopped further work and it was not until afterwards when the Council built some prefabricated houses for homeless families that New Addington really began to expand to what it is today with its own factory estate. Published by George Kennie.

Don Bowles & his Croydon Accordion Band 1936

Dance bands for private functions were much in demand although the taste for accordions may have been declining by the mid-1930s, the date of this publicity postcard. Obviously Don Bowles was a prize-winning band as it had won second prize in an All Britain contest. At this time Don Bowles kept a musical instrument shop at 284 High Street, Croydon. Publisher not known.

Croydon Repertory Theatre, Garden Party 3rd July 1937

This was at no. 23 Wellesley Road in one of the houses that remained between Whitgift Middle School and Poplar Walk. There was enough space for a small garden party behind the house. The Repertory Theatre operated for a few years in the 1930s until the Second World War when it was badly damaged. Publisher not known.

Brighton Road, Purley, about 1935

The Astoria was one of two 1930s cinemas in Purley and it is seen here when the advertised films were 'Orchids To You' and 'Last Days of Pompeii'. The building has been replaced by Astoria Court, home to a solicitor on the corner of Whytecliffe Road South. On its northern side can be seen Carr's Garage, also demolished. The paved area between Brighton Road and High Street for many years contained an open ditch for the Bourne. Published by C.H.Price.

Ice Rink Purley, 1938

The Imperial Ice Rink was a great attraction at 112 Brighton Road, Purley situated in the 1930s parade south of Grovelands Road. This postcard of an enthusiastic looking staff and manager was used to promote the ice rink in 1938. It was later replaced by the Orchid Ballroom and other dance halls and night clubs before changing to the present fitness centre and health club. Photographed by Archie Handford and presumably published by the Imperial Ice Rink.

Bourne & Balmer (Croydon) Ltd., Dingwall Road in the 1930s

Bourne & Balmer had an office at 97 George Street and around 1933 had erected a coach station in Dingwall Road near East Croydon Station. This was an imposing building and the firm became the most active of the Croydon coach firms. Photograph by Howard M. King. Publisher not known but presumably Bourne & Balmer.

Northcote Road, Croydon. Lobb's Corner

An interesting feature of the trolleybus system was the central wire with lights in the overhead system at road junctions which was used to guide the drivers should fog make navigation difficult. It was very important that trolleybus drivers were careful to follow a course that avoided dewirement and possible damage to the overhead wires. Published by C.H. Price.

Whitgift Hospital, Croydon

This ancient building somewhat miraculously remains in the very centre of Croydon in spite of several past attempts to have it demolished. It was founded by the Archbishop of Canterbury, John Whitgift, and we know that building work began on 17th January 1596. However due to bad weather the foundation stone could not be laid until 22nd March 1596, which is therefore remembered as Founder's Day. The building was completed on 29th September 1599. One can get a good view of the quadrangle from the restaurant at the top of Allders' department store but the building can also be visited at times. Published by C.H. Price. This may have been his last commercial postcard as it was published in 1939, the year the 59B bus route started running.

1939 TO 1959

A.R.P. Mobile First Aid Unit

Croydon Council operated this mobile first aid unit as part of its Auxiliary Ambulance Service. Eight first aid posts had been set up and then three mobile ones. Initially they were based at Mayday Hospital. Vans had been converted to enable help to be given in distant parts of Croydon and they had a folding operating table and emergency lighting and were manned by a doctor and at least four other staff. Publisher not known.

Salvage Waste Collection Van

A salvage campaign was started in November 1939 and collections introduced. There was house-to-house canvassing for waste paper, rags, bottles, bones and metal. In addition, special collecting shops were opened. In 1941, feeding stuff for pigs and poultry was needed so collecting bins were placed by roads. There were also salvage drives with vehicles with speakers, rather like an update of the rag and bone-man system. As the war continued, every house had been given a waste paper sack and unwanted books were also actively sought. Special exhibitions and events were also held. Publisher not known.

Corporation Methane Gas-powered Tanker

A new system of sewage treatment introduced in Croydon in 1938 produced methane gas but no real use was made of it then. However with the scarcity of petrol, a need arose for this gas and fortunately the Borough Engineer had been astute for he, somewhat ironically, adapted a machine he had seen earlier in Germany in 1935 and managed to produce fuel for Council lorries. The gas was stored in cylinders on the vehicles and after trials, it was fitted to over sixty lorries. It was recorded that over the war years, 85,000 gallons of petrol was saved by this method. Publisher not known.

Crystal Palace Tower demolition in 1941

The Crystal Palace, that Victorian masterpiece of engineering and design by Joseph Paxton, had been built for the Great Exhibition of 1851 in London's Hyde Park. It was later taken down and rebuilt in an enlarged form at Upper Norwood and became the venue for many exhibitions, events of all sorts, concerts and such things as balloon flights. Unfortunately it was burnt down on the night of 30th November 1936. The 284 foot high North Tower remained as one of the few reminders of this great building but was demolished on 16th April 1941 to prevent it being too much of a navigation aid to German pilots. Publisher not known.

"Made in Germany - Finished In England" August 1940

This Messerschmitt M.E. 109 aeroplane had been shot down that summer in a Surrey cornfield when the wounded pilot was able to land before he died. It was on show in the Fairfield car park for ten days in August 1940 and a fee charged in aid of the Croydon Fighter Plane Fund. The area in which the plane was sited was below the level of Park Lane and had been created when gravel was extracted. The land was thus already levelled for the post-war rebuilding of this area and space for car parking. The Southern Railway Bowling Club had a green in this spot up to the mid-1930s before moving to Plough Lane, Waddon. The former Fire Station is prominent behind the Messerschmitt. Published by The Croydon Times.

"MADE IN GERMANY — FINISHED IN ENGLAND."
MESSERSCHMITT M.E.109.
ALL PROCEEDS GO TO OUR LOCAL SPITFIRE FUND.

C.T. Photo.

A.R.P. Squad

Air Raid Precaution staff ready for action in the daytime although much of their work was inevitably at night. Many wardens were unpaid but some paid staff had to be recruited at times. Many wardens' posts were in rooms in private houses reinforced with sandbags so this postcard is quite typical. Generally there were some 5,000 wardens in Croydon of which 4,500 were volunteers. Publisher not known.

Waldronhyrst Hotel, South Croydon 1940s

This large Victorian house, 24 The Waldrons, was always called Waldronhyrst. Around 1896 it was bought by John Lane Densham and was extended in time so that a staff of ten was then needed including a coachman. Densham was a member of a big tea firm and it was he that coined the name of Mazawattee Tea in 1887. This tea was widely advertised and very popular for many years. A large head office was built at Tower Hill, London and an extensive factory at New Cross. Unfortunately both buildings were badly damaged by bombing in the Second World War although parts of the New Cross factory can still be spotted by the eagle-eyed from passing trains. After Densham died in South Africa, Waldronhyrst became a residential hotel and mention is made on this postcard of its deep underground air raid shelter. It was demolished in the 1970s and the area is now a large housing estate. Publisher not known.

Parish Church, Croydon 1946

The main Croydon St. George's Day Parade held on 23rd April 1946, which is the traditional date for the death of St. George in 303 A.D. Scouts from all over the town marched to the Parish Church of St. John the Baptist. Published by The Croydon Times.

Kennards of Croydon 1945

The Peace Decorations for V.E. (Victory in Europe) Day on 8th May 1945 which the store claimed to be unrivalled anywhere in Britain. Certainly on this rather garish postcard, it could not have been missed easily. Kennards was one of the three department stores in Croydon, the others being Allders on the opposite side of North End and Grants in High Street. It had started back in 1853 and grew fast .On the back of the card is the following: "Known everywhere as 'The Store where the Bargains come from'. Leading London Suburban Store of 150 departments covering 8¾ acres and employing staff of 1,350. Famous for its wide range of ever-changing Merchandise, Attractions and lavish Entertainments, Mecca of the Stars of Stage, Screen and Radio." Publisher presumably Kennards.

Croydon, High Street, 1946

A view to the north with Surrey Street ahead on the left. The photograph was taken shortly after WWII. There is very little traffic and the windows of a few shops have temporary fittings, a legacy of air-raid damage or precautions. The trams are passing the Davis Theatre (right). Published by The Croydon Times.

Norwood Lake, 1946

This is now South Norwood Lake and is the only large expanse of water in Croydon. It was constructed as a reservoir for the Croydon Canal in the early 1800s. The canal was closed and bought by the London & Croydon Railway Company in 1836 which used the canal route. The lake became derelict until 1881 when it was opened as part of a sports club. The area was later opened to the public. The motor-boat, The Skylark, provided trips around the lake for a few years after the Second World War. Published by The Croydon Times.

Sylvan Estate, Upper Norwood about 1946

A rare postcard of prefabricated houses. These were introduced after 1944 as a result of the Ministry of Works Emergency Factory Made housing programme and whole estates were built for people made homeless and by slum clearance schemes. By 1948, about 160,000 had been erected in the U.K.. They were bungalows and were primarily meant for families. They had two bedrooms, a bathroom with a bath, a separate W.C. which was unusual then, a living room and a kitchen. They were made of steel, aluminium, timber and asbestos, depending on the type. Although they were only temporary homes and planned to last for about ten years, some still remain today in certain parts of England. Published by Skilton.

THORNTON HEATH. C.T.149

Thornton Heath, 1946

This view to the west shows only two vehicles and a tram in Brigstock Road. There is also a visible sign of German bomb damage as a whole run of buildings has been demolished on the far left although the publisher made some slight strokes to mask it. There is little activity in the area. Published by The Croydon Times.

NORTH END, CROYDON. (CROYDON TIMES COPYRIGHT) CT29

North End, Croydon, 1946

There is little action here either although there are a few trams. A poster for the nearby Civic Hall Lunchtime Concerts (formerly the Brotherhood Hall) is on the left. The 16th century Whitgift Hospital was quite badly damaged in the war but this is not obvious in this view. Published by The Croydon Times.

SNOWDRIFT CROYDON. 1948.

Snowdrift, Croydon - 1948

Three snowbound travellers pose for a photograph in front of a Hall & Co's van in February 1948. Several other motor cars are abandoned in the snowdrifts along Limpsfield Road, Chelsham. Just outside the borough, this road (Croydon to Westerham) is the highest main road in the South of England. The photographer was looking south with Beech Farm and outbuildings along the line of Beech Farm Road. Unlike the snowdrifts of the previous winter, the 1948 snow disappeared within a week. Publisher not known.

Church Road, Upper Norwood

Another quiet scene with little traffic visible. The Century Cinema at 18 Church Road is the nearer cinema and was built in 1930 as the Albany. It became the Century in 1950 but closed in 1958. The building remains but is now boarded up. The second one, the Granada, was the Rialto in 1928 but changed name in 1950 up to 1968 when it was used for bingo. It is now closed and an application for change of use has been submitted. Published by F. Frith & Co. Ltd.

Sandpits Road, Shirley

Sandpits Road runs east from Upper Shirley Road and was known mostly as the base of John Bennett, Shirley's oldest family business which was behind the camera in this picture. It had started in 1777 in Wickham Road selling sand and this developed into making and selling birch brooms. A move was then made to Sandpits Road where sand, peat, loam, manure and shrubs were sold for many years. It closed in the late 1980s. The Sandrock Hotel is at the far left of this picture which probably dates from the 1950s. Published by F. Frith & Co. Ltd.

The Village, Addington

The village facing east before modem development took place. On the left are buildings of Home Farm, with the Church of St. Mary the Blessed Virgin in the distance, the oldest building which probably dates from 1080. Five 19th century archbishops of Canterbury are buried there. Published by F. Frith & Co. Ltd.

CROYDON, GEORGE STREET. V4810

Croydon, George Street

Some cars are on the roads at last by the late 1940s, together with a new no.12 RT type bus. There is still a poster for National Savings outside the Public Halls. These were built in the 1860s by the Croydon Literary & Scientific Society and were a useful venue for many cultural organisations and for musical events, exhibitions and a library. They were also the first home of the Croydon Art School. The prominent clock-tower was that of Thrift's Grocery Warehouse which was demolished in 1962. Published by The Photochrom Company Ltd.

CY 2 CROYDON. NORTH END

Croydon, North End about 1953

A view to the north with the front of Kennards store on the left with pedestrians mainly here. The old tram tracks have been removed and the road re-asphalted which was done around 1952. The entrance to Whitgift Middle School is on the right. Published by A. Mason.

The Flats, New Addington

It was not until the Council built some prefabricated houses after the Second World War that New Addington really began to expand to what it is today together with its own factory estate. This postcard shows some of the post-war flats. Published by F. Frith & Co. Ltd.

1960 TO 2010

OLD CROYDON
Looking North from Pitlake Bridge 12.3.1960

COLLECTORCARD © Croydon CR0 1HW 1974 C1505

Old Croydon in 1960

The 630 trolleybus route replaced the trams in 1937 and it is a little surprising that although trolleybuses ran in the town for 25 years, only one contemporary postcard is known to show one (see page 80). This view looking north from Pitlake Bridge was totally changed by the construction of the Roman Way Flyover in the 1970s. Published by Pamlin Prints.

M3415 LAST DAYS ON THE WOODSIDE - SANDERSTEAD LINE
Leaving Coombe Lane Tunnel 26.4.1983

Pamlin Prints Croydon CR0 1HW © 1983

Last days on the Woodside - Sanderstead Line, 1983

The Woodside and South Croydon line was never very successful as it merely skirted the built up area of Croydon. Several attempts were made by British Railways to close it, successfully in 1983. This view shows a two-car electric unit leaving Coombe Lane Tunnel on its way to Sanderstead. The trackbed and tunnels now form part of the Tramlink route to New Addington. Published by Pamlin Prints.

M2481 CROYDON AT WAR
South Croydon Bus Garage after Air Raid 11.4.1941
(Photo: S. Quilter) (Centre ST 882, Right STL 371)

Pamlin Prints Croydon CR0 1HW

Croydon at War, 1941

The virtual destruction of Croydon Bus Garage with the loss of 65 buses in 1941 was one of the worst incidents to be suffered by London Transport. Several staff were killed. It would not have been possible to publish a postcard with such a view at the time because of strict censorship regulations. Published by Pamlin Prints.

BRIGHTON ROAD, PURLEY

Brighton Road, Purley - about 1972

This is the view looking north up the Brighton Road from Purley Cross Roads. It a fine example of the small number of high-quality topographical postcards published by Pamlin Prints.

Katharine Street, Croydon about 1890

This is one of a series of 24 Local history Postcards published by a small group of members of The Bourne and CNHSS Societies. A visit was made to Frith's premises in Reigate and a selection made from their original glass-plate negatives. They were in all probability the last real photographic cards produced by the company as it was in the process of liquidation and closed shortly afterwards. The view is looking west along Katharine Street with the Central Croydon Station cutting on the left. This now forms part of The Queen's Gardens. The old Second Town Hall in the High Street can be seen in the distance.

Sylvan Hill, Upper Norwood about 1899

Emile Zola was exiled from France in 1898 and stayed for some time with his wife at The Queen's Hotel in Church Road. He was fascinated by the area and spent a good deal of time indulging his hobby of photography. This is an example of his work showing roadworks in Sylvan Hill, by the corner of Church Road. One of a series of postcards produced by the Emile Zola Society in 1998.

Whitgift Centre, Croydon C.084002L

Whitgift Centre, Croydon

The Centre was built on the site of the former Whitgift Middle School after it had transferred to new buildings at Shirley Park in 1965. The Centre was built in two stages in 1966 and 1970 and officially opened in October 1970. In 1986 a major refurbishment scheme began which was also carried out in stages. The Forum public house was demolished and the whole centre enclosed. Photograph by J. Banks. Published by E.T.W. Dennis & Sons Ltd.

A view from Addington Hills

This autumnal picture highlights the Croydon skyline contrasted with the large area of woodland. Addington Hills is more generally known locally as Shirley Hills. Published by J. Arthur Dixon.

Queen's Gardens, Croydon C.084001L

Queen's Gardens, Croydon

Work started on these gardens in October 1982 and was finished in the Spring of 1983 in time for the Borough Centenary celebrations. They were opened by Her Majesty Queen Elizabeth II on 21 st June 1983. The site had been that of the former Police Station and adjacent land and incorporated the 1896 Town Hall Gardens. Published by Dennis.

High Street, Croydon in 1883

This faces north. The road was widened in the 1890s as part of the major rebuilding scheme. The sign of 'The Greyhound' hotel is a prominent reminder of the days when coaches passed here daily and publicises its post-horse facility. It is very clear why the road needed widening but the town lost some of its character as a result. Published by CNHSS.

Whitgift Hospital and North End 1945

A rare colour photograph dating from 1945 and a reminder of the days when traffic used this route as a through road. The old type of tram (route 42) retains its wartime white painted fender and the 68 bus has some windows boarded up. The flags on Allders store celebrate V.J. Day (Victory in Japan). Photograph taken by Harold Bennett, who was a pilot in Coastal Command and fortunately came home from Canada with some good quality film - not available in the U.K. until the late 1950s. Published by CNHSS.

Aerial view of Park Lane and the Underpass and the Fairfield Halls about 1980.

An unusual night-time view. Work on the underpass began in 1962. The Fairfield Halls opened in 1962 and are the town's main venue for theatre, music and events. Photograph taken by Phil Ray. Published by Croydon Press & Public Relations Office.

Battle of Britain Memorial, Purley Way 1991

This large monument is on the west side of Purley Way to the south of Airport House. It was built as a tribute to all connected with Croydon and its aerodrome who died in the air or on the ground in the Second World War. It was unveiled on 27th October 1991. Photograph by Tom Samson. Published by the Croydon Airport Society.

The Town Crier at Croydon's Forestry and Country Fayre at Selsdon Wood

A pleasant link to the past; Dick Hill, the Croydon Town Crier, at Selsdon Wood. This post was created by the management of the Fairfield Halls. Photograph by Sheila Lovell. Published by Sheltie Cards.

Selsdon, Surrey - late 1980s

Addington Road, Selsdon with a 64 bus going to Thornton Heath Garage. Photograph by Sheila Lovell. Published by Sheltie Cards.

Croydon aerial view

A view from the 1990s. Here we can see at the top the railway line passing East Croydon Station, the Fairfield Halls at centre right slightly obscured by Tabemer House, and the proliferation of office blocks together with the Whitgift Centre along Wellesley Road. The flyover is at the lower right corner. Photograph by Handford for Croydon Hotels Association. Published by J. Arthur Dixon.

Croham Hurst, Croydon

This is a view to the east highlighting the large expanse of woodland and open country still remaining to the south of Croydon. Photograph by Tom Samson. Published by CNHSS.

Purley looking towards High street - 1995

The tall, modern office block on the left dominates the busy road system near Purley Cross Roads. The roads shown are, from the left, Purley Road, High Street, Whytecliffe Road South and Godstone Road. The office block bears no name or number and is home to a computer company. It replaced the Railway Hotel with its distinctive dome bar easily visible from the railway. The photographer was standing in the approach to Tesco looking towards a 1930s building housing Touche, a ladies' hairdresser on the site of a baker and confectioner. In the centre of the postcard is Mafeking Terrace, High Street. Published by the Bourne Society.

Bourne Flood, Whyteleafe, December 2000

The Bourne has caused a flood on the A22 at Whyteleafe. The photograph was taken looking south towards the left-hand turn for Maple Road and there is evidence of small boats as well as sandbags and boarding to protect the shops. The Bourne on this occasion caused this busy road to be closed for a month and traffic had to be re-routed via Warlingham. A rising of the Bourne is traditionally thought to predict a national disaster and this flooding was followed by the serious outbreak of foot and mouth disease. Note the price of petrol at the garage! Published by the Bourne Society.

Kenley Station - 1989

The station master's house at Kenley Station with its steep gables and tall chimney stacks is the most attractive building on the Caterham railway line. It dates from 1856 when the line was opened and there was a similar building at Caterham Station but this was demolished in 1899. The Kenley building's future is uncertain following a period of use as a kindergarten but a blue plaque notes its impressive history. The trees on the slopes of Riddlesdown contrast noticeably with old photographs that show smooth, open downland with hardly a tree to be seen. Published by the Bourne Society.

Croydon Tramlink 2000

The first Croydon Tramlink tram making a journey under power was on 16th June 1999 but the actual services began to New Addington on 10th May 2000, followed by that to Beckenham on 23rd May and Wimbledon on 30th May 2000. Car no. 2543 is passing through Lloyd Park in the Spring of 2002. The estate here had been owned by Frank Lloyd. He was a newspaper magnate whose father had founded Lloyd's News. Frank Lloyd lived at Coombe House for 35 years and after his death in 1927 the land eventually came to the Council so that there is now 114 acres of open land in addition to many other open spaces to the east and the south of the town. This was the original tram livery. Photograph by J.F. Bradshaw. Published by Transport of Delight.

Wellesley Road, Croydon

Looking north from the George Street junction. The underpass built in the 1960s carries traffic under this junction to the north and south. A tram can be seen on the right approaching south along Wellesley Road. Photograph by John Gent. Published by CNHSS.

Selsdon Park Hotel about 1980

This is a rear view of Selsdon's most famous building. Inside this imposing hotel is the core of an old house which was converted to a gentleman's mansion and estate around 1810. It was soon enlarged in the Gothic style by George Smith who lived here for much of the 19th century. A later owner was Wickham Noakes, a brewer, who often organised shooting parties here. In 1924 it was bought by Allan Doble Sanderson, a businessman and racing driver, who converted it to a 24-bedroomed hotel in 1925. He wasted little time and by 1935 had added large east and west wings and encased the whole structure in red brick to give it a neo-Jacobean look. A golf course was constructed in 1929. Since then, there have been other extensions together with a leisure centre. The grounds cover over 200 acres. The hotel is now part of the 'Principal Hayley Group'.

Croydon Church and Archbishops Palace - 2007

The Great Hall of the Old Palace is on the left and The Parish Church is on the right. This is an excellent example of a church and manor house occupying adjacent sites for centuries. Croydon is very fortunate to have retained this feature. Six archbishops of Canterbury are buried in the church, and the palace is now part of the Whitgift School and is probably the oldest building in the country to house a school.

At the end of February 2011 it was announced that the church would be designated a Minster at the end of May in recognition of its importance. Photograph by John Gent - published by CNHSS.

Acknowledgements

The Editor and the Council of **CNHSS** (Croydon Natural History & Scientific Society) gratefully acknowledge the help of the Assistant Editors, Ken Harman and Roger Packham, in the production of this publication. Unfortunately the names of most of the original photographers, and many of the publishers are not known but their efforts have recorded many scenes and places before and during the great changes of the twentieth century which altered the area irrevocably.

All the postcards are reproduced from the collection of John Gent, with the exception of those of Roffey & Clark's Lending Library (page 5), and the Circus Parade in North End (page 47) which are from Ken Harman's collection.

It has not been possible to identify or contact the holders of copyright where this still exists but due acknowledgement is given to them and to John Bradshaw (JB Cards); Richard Gibb and the Press Department of Croydon Council; Tom Samson and Handford Photography; Croydon Libraries and Croydon Museum and Arts; Sheila Lovell (Sheltie Cards) and The Zola Society. Thanks are due also to Tim Harding who has identified some vehicles and assisted with dating of some images, and to Terry Cooper, Susan Gilbert, Elizabeth Malarkey, Michael Noone and Richard Norman for general assistance.

The Editor has collected postcards for 75 years and has, since the 1960s, attended many Postcard Fairs. He has appreciated the help and friendship of numerous dealers and fellow-collectors who have helped him to expand his collection. A special mention is due to Roy and Cheryl Allen, Julian Dunn, Brian Girling, John Holder, Brian and Mary Lund, Ron Meads and Dave Smith (Memories of Hendon).

Selected Reading

Byatt, Anthony	Picture Postcards and their Publishers Golden Age Postcard Books 1978
Godden, Geoffrey	Collecting Picture Postcards Phillimore & Co Ltd 1996
Holt, Tonie and Valmai	Picture Postcards of the Golden Age MacGibbon & Kee 1971
Marshall, Lawrence	O.J. Morris's Southern Railways 1919-1959 Middleton Press 1997

Local directories published by Gray, Warren and Ward from 1851 onwards, and local newspapers from 1855 are invaluable sources of information. The Local Studies Library and Archive at the Clocktower in Katharine Street holds a vast stock of illustrations, publications and records for reference purposes.

A regular monthly magazine, **Picture Postcard Monthly**, edited by Brian and Mary Lund is published by Reflections of a Bygone Age, 15 Debdale Lane, Keyworth, Nottingham NG12 5HT. They also publish a **Picture Postcard Annual** each Autumn. Both publications contain extremely interesting and useful articles about postcards and publishers.

Picture Postcard Values is an annual publication, usually published in the Autumn. It contains a great deal of useful information about postcards and gives some indication of values.

Postcard Fairs are held regularly and widely around the country. A visit to one of these is a good way of starting a collection.